Hob‹

Memoirs of
Travel and Adventure

Capt. William J. Wright, USMC (Ret.)

VANTAGE PRESS
New York

Jack Wright

Cover design by Sue Thomas

FIRST EDITION

All rights reserved, including the right of
reproduction in whole or in part in any form.

Copyright © 2002 by Capt. William J. Wright, USMC (Ret.)

Published by Vantage Press, Inc.
516 West 34th Street, New York, New York 10001

Manufactured in the United States of America
ISBN: 0-533-14073-0

Library of Congress Catalog Card No.: 01-126925

0 9 8 7 6 5 4 3 2 1

With love and gratitude

To my beloved wife, Elaine Hyde Wright,
truly my better half since August 16, 1942

and
To my parents, Lee and Essie Thomas Wright,
who did a great job of raising six sons and three daughters

and
To my sister, Annie Laura Aaron,
who made it possible with her expert transcribing skills
to turn my scribbled notes into a real manuscript

Contents

Foreword

My brother Jack Wright was always an early riser, beginning as a young boy when he had to get up at four o'clock in the morning to milk the cows. Later, in the United States Marine Corps, he had to get up at the sound of reveille, so he never got in the habit of sleeping late. Now at age eighty-five, when he could have slept long past five-thirty, he still got out of bed and got dressed.

Until recently, he and his wife lived in the country. He liked getting up early then because he could walk to the pond and feed the fish and pet geese. He could pick vegetables from the garden. He could hike through the woods. But all that had changed after they sold the farm and moved to the condominium. Now after he drank his second cup of coffee, read the newspaper and worked the crossword puzzle, there just wasn't much to do. His passion for reading had always been a big part of his life but recently this pleasure was curtailed when glaucoma took the sight of one eye.

Then, early one morning, something happened. He picked up a number two pencil and lined notebook paper and started to write. The more he wrote, the more he remembered. He recalled what it was like living on a small farm with his parents and five brothers and three sisters. He could envision the one-room, one-teacher schoolhouse where he started to school, and the excitement that came with learning to read. He even picked up scraps of paper in the cotton fields and read the words on them. In high school he hid Zane Grey novels in his text books and continued to read until the teacher caught him. All of this reading gave him the notion to run away from the farm and travel for adventure. He learned to hop freight trains and sell magazines enabling him to visit every state in the United States before he joined the Marines at age twenty-one. He tells of the serendipitous way in which he met his beloved wife-to-be, Elaine Hyde, while training in Florida.

He amuses us with recollections of church revivals, box suppers, ice cream suppers, and the many ways we entertained ourselves before the days of electricity, radio and television.

His early military career gave him the opportunity to be in China before World War II and also after the war. He describes his three years of combat in the Pacific, and also his tour of duty in Korea. He recalls life after military retirement when he returned to his homeland in rural South Carolina, raised cattle, worked in real estate, and also served in the South Carolina Legislature.

Although his formal education was cut short, being an avid reader and traveler, Jack became self-educated. After twenty years in the USMC, he retired as Captain in 1957.

This book provides entertainment for all ages. Those who were too young to know about the Great Depression will learn how people not only survived hard times but also found ways to enjoy life to the fullest. The older generation will enjoy revisiting those times and will relate, maybe in some cases with nostalgia, to the places they have been. From horse and buggy days to twenty-first century technology, there is much to remember and much to tell.

Annie Laura Aaron

Part I

1

Summer on the Farm

The Lee Wright home place, Anderson County, South Carolina

I was born in the Piedmont section of South Carolina on July 6, 1915. It was Dixie all right, but it wasn't frosty. July is a hot, miserable month, but better times were ahead. We farmers would call it lay-by time. The cotton would have reached most of its growth. There would be blooms, white when they first opened but turning red by the next day. When most of the work was done we would chop cotton a final time and usually plow to get rid of the grass and weeds.

It was then that the good times started. For about three or four weeks we would do only the necessary chores and we didn't have to go out in the fields to work. When I was a boy we always built a "wash hole," which was a place to get together with our buddies to swim and play. This pool was made by damming up a small stream. It wouldn't get over four or five feet deep, but it was cool. The first big rain would break the dam. We could replace it or just let it go if summer was about over. There were plenty of things to do. We could fish or seine, hike in the woods, and climb trees. One of our fun activities was stealing watermelons. This seemed unnecessary since we all had melons at home, but the fascination was the strategic planning and carrying out the operation, including how to reach the watermelons without being seen. We studied the situation and planned ways to approach from the woods or creep up a gully. It might be necessary to crawl part of the way. When we secured the melons we would place them in a spring or stream to get them cool, and they tasted so good.

There were revival meetings in nearby churches, sometimes called protracted services. Preaching lasted from eleven-thirty to one o'clock, and preachers told us about hell and damnation. This was also a time for young boys and girls to socialize. It was even OK to sit together if you were not too bashful. Many romances started at that little church, and some led to marriage and family. Also this was a time for company dinners. It was considered an honor to have the preacher come to dinner, and when he came there would be others with him. That meant kids would have a second or third wait for tables. Only the best was good enough for these important people. At this time of year we had a beautiful supply of wonderful fresh vegetables, including corn, peas, beans, okra, squash, tomatoes, and more. Almost everything in the garden would be ready to eat, including watermelons and cantaloupes. The cured ham that we had been keeping for special occasions would be served. There would be fried chicken, cakes, and pies. We had been eating fatback up until this time, so the ham was really a treat. After all the folks had finished eating and rested for a while the watermelons were cut. These had been cooling in large tin tubs filled with well water, which was always cool. We got lots of exercise from drawing up buckets of water with a rope and windlass.

We were back in church that night. In addition to the preaching there would be singing. Visiting groups would be there and this used up some of the time, but an hour or so of the sermon was usually the rule.

2

Summer Ends and Fall Begins

All of this ended in mid-August. It was time to pull corn fodder. We removed the leaves, tied them in a bundle, and left them to cure out. I don't think there was much food value, but it was just a filler for the mules in winter to go along with the corn. After that we got ready to make molasses. We stripped the molasses stalks and cut them down with a scythe, removed the top that contained the seed, loaded the stalks on the wagon, and hauled them to the molasses mill.

Since I had three older brothers I was usually a helper, who got the jobs that others didn't want. On one occasion, though, when I was about twelve I had a very important job that made me feel like I was becoming a man. I got up at two o'clock in the morning, caught the mule and rode about a mile to the molasses mill, and started the process of grinding the stalks to squeeze out the juice. When my uncle arrived he would start the cooking. The grinding was accomplished with a mule pulling a sweep that went in circles. The juice was collected and then transferred to the cooking pans.We had to start the grinding very early in order to have the juice ready to cook at daylight. With all this labor we would produce forty to fifty gallons of molasses. If there was a surplus we would sell a gallon for forty to fifty cents, but usually there wasn't much left over to sell. We kept a jar of molasses on the kitchen table and it didn't last long. Everybody liked molasses on hot biscuits or cornbread.

About two weeks later we would be in the cotton field. Every boll of cotton had to be picked by hand. It couldn't be picked until it was fully open, so we picked cotton over a period of several weeks. Some of the bolls would be punctured by boll weevils, and this made them harder to gather. School started about the first of October, but farm work had priority over school. After the cotton was picked there were still things that had to be done. We pulled corn, dug up sweet potatoes, and hilled them for the winter. A sweet potato bed was made ready by placing cornstalks like a teepee and then covered with dirt. We had potatoes for several months and often carried a baked sweet potato in our school lunches. All of the cooking was done on a wood stove, which meant we had to get up a year's supply of wood. The wood had to be cured out before it made a good fire for cooking. All of the woodcutting was done with axes and it took lots of time, but there was time left for fun things, too.

Almost everyone had hunting dogs. We usually had beagles, and they were better for tracking rabbits because they could manage to get into places where a larger dog couldn't go. There were usually two or three packs of dogs at a hunt. The hunters could recognize their dogs' barks and cheered them on by calling out their names. A swamp or wooded area would be surrounded by hunters, and the dogs would try to locate the rabbits and chase them out so the hunters could get a shot. Rabbits are good to eat, especially the wild ones, and no game was ever wasted. Rabbits caught in a gum were better to eat because there would not be any shot in them. The reason they were called gums probably was because originally they were made out of a hollowed-out log cut from a gum tree. There were not enough logs that were suitable, so we made them out of boards. Trapping started in November and lasted about three months. We would check every morning, usually about daylight. If we caught more rabbits than we needed, they would be sold or traded for something we did need. Most of the time we traded for shotgun shells.

We had to be early risers to get everything done. On a winter day I would get up around four in the morning, build a fire in the cook stove, and also start a fire in the fireplace. Usually there were enough live coals that had been covered up with ashes the night before to make it easy to get a fire going. After that I would go to the barn and milk the cow. We ate breakfast about six o'clock and then gathered up our book satchels and lunch bags and headed off for the schoolhouse.

When we got through picking cotton we could pick for our neighbors if they needed help. We got about forty cents per hundred pounds of cotton and could earn about eighty cents per day. This would give us a little spending money for the county fair, which was one of the big occasions of the year. Actually, it was the carnival that interested the young folks. There were rides, sideshows, and hot dogs. Most of the years they had free performances.

3

Thanksgiving and Christmas Holidays

After the fair we looked forward to Thanksgiving. Relatives visited back and forth and enjoyed lots of good food. In the early morning the men and boys would go rabbit hunting. (*There was no big game left at that time, but now there has been a comeback and deer and wild turkeys are plentiful. Beavers have been reintroduced and have caused lots of flooding, but these ponds have provided places for ducks and other wildlife.*)

The next thing we looked forward to was Christmas. We had no expensive toys, but we were happier on Christmas morning than children are today when they get so much all year. If it was a good year we might get a pocketknife, cap pistol, or harmonica. Our stockings would have a variety of fruits, nuts, and candy. Special memories include the wonderful smell of tangerines, oranges, apples, bananas, grapes, and raisins still on the stems—fruits that were not plentiful until Christmas morning.

In our community fireworks were a big part of the Christmas celebration—more so than the Fourth of July—and we had lots of fireworks. Getting together with neighbors and kinfolk was a big thing. For a couple of weeks during Christmas no one did farm work and folks did a lot of visiting. Cousins would come or we would go visit them and stay two or three days and nights. Dances were held almost every night. Each night they would announce where the next one would be. The music was a fiddle and banjo and sometimes other instruments. Sometimes a few people would get loaded on moonshine whiskey and would start fights or damage property. *It got so bad later that people quit having dances at their homes. There was a fellow called Bad Eye. I never knew his real name. Almost everyone was afraid of him. I was in a place one night, and Bad Eye and a few others were gambling with dice. Two deputies walked into the room, and when they saw Bad Eye they turned and left the room. I have heard that he would ride his mule on the sidewalk and the police wouldn't do anything about it. They finally solved the problem by hiring him on the police force.*

There was a lot of baking going on during this festive time. Mama put us to work grating fresh coconuts and picking out nuts. By the time Christmas came we had cakes of every variety. The cupboard in the dining room was loaded with goodies that had irresistible looks and smells. They were safe because the temperature in that room was always cold and because we knew better than to go near them. This was one time the cupboard was anything but bare.

At the schoolhouse there was usually a Christmas play and there would be a tree. We couldn't have lights because there was no electricity. We would take axes and look for a holly tree with red berries. Popcorn would be threaded on strings and placed on the branches. Most of the parents would attend this special event. In addition to the plays put on by the children, we had cake walks and box suppers. The girls would prepare a basket or box filled with good things to eat. The boys would bid on them. A girl would whisper a description of her box or basket to her boyfriend, so he would bid on hers and then they would get to eat together. Sometimes two boys would want the same box and the bidding would get out of hand because one boy didn't want the other fellow eating with his girl. Any money raised by these endeavors went to support the school and pay the teacher, who got paid about seventy dollars a month.

4

My Early Education

I started to school in a one-room schoolhouse, and it was heated by a coal stove. The drinking water was brought in with buckets from a spring, and we drank from a community dipper; later on we were encouraged to furnish our own cups. One of the teachers told me years later that usually there were about seventy students and of course they could not be seated if they all came on the same day. She said this problem was solved by having older students take a class to the cloakroom. There were two cloakrooms, one for the girls and the other for boys. The boys all dressed alike: bibbed overalls, a work shirt, and shoes or boots but barefoot most of the year. The girls had simple cotton dresses. There were no contests to try to outdress one another as I recall. When I started school there were ten grades. Most of the students didn't get that far. They were working on the farm by that time. There was no bussing, so most of the boys quit around the eighth grade. My older brothers did not go to town to the upper grades because it was too far to walk. About two years before I got to the eighth grade they started bussing students to high school, and then there were eleven grades. Very few made it to college. Most of the students either farmed or got a job in a cotton mill. This was hard work at low pay, but there was housing for the worker and a payday every week. Most farmers preferred to stay in the country even if they had less income. There was something about being independent. It felt good to be your own boss.

I had not been doing well in school and had not completed the tenth grade. At that time there were only eleven grades. I had trouble with one teacher, and he wanted to give me a few licks with a ruler. I wouldn't let him and after that I thought it would be better if I changed schools. There was a country school that still carried all eleven grades. It was about a two-mile walk, but I had company most of the way. Two old maid sisters ran the school, and they ruled with an iron hand. Their names were Lula and Emma. They would whip anyone they thought needed it, no matter what size. I was a new boy, and I had to prove myself. I had a fight with a bully who was bigger than me, but I made out all right. This showed that I wouldn't be run over. There was a little country grocery store about a quarter of a mile from the schoolhouse. The boys dared me to go to the store while school was in session, so of course, I went. I sneaked back and thought I had gotten away with it. I believe somebody told the teacher about me. They wanted to see me get a whipping. They were not disappointed. Miss Lula laid it on. I guess this was part of the initiation. After that I was considered a regular fellow and didn't have any more difficulties. A lot of the older boys only attended school when there wasn't anything else to do. They quit as soon as the farming started.

*   *   *

Part II

5

Boarding School in North Georgia

My mother could see that I wasn't doing well in school, and she was determined to have her children stay in school as long as possible. She knew that farming was a hard way to earn a living, and she never encouraged any of us to stay on the farm.

My mother's birthplace was in North Georgia, and she had lived there until she was twelve years old. She still had relatives there, and she heard about a boarding school where students could work their way through school. In 1932 the entire nation was in a deep depression. I don't know how my mother managed to get up the few dollars needed for admission to the boarding school in North Georgia, but she made arrangements for me to be admitted. She also got up a few good clothes for me to wear to school. It was a year-round school, and I reported in about the first of August 1932. They had not started classroom work, but the farming was going on.

The school owned lots of good land and lots of brick buildings. They must have been heavily endowed. They had a dairy and a barn for the livestock. Mules were used for plowing; there were no tractors. It was a place where poor mountain girls and boys could get a high school education. I plowed corn and worked in the dairy. It wasn't heavy work, and there were lots of workers. When we were off duty we could wander around the area. We could walk to the nearest

17

town, Clayton, Georgia, or we could climb mountains. They were not very high, but I had never seen any real mountains and I was impressed. We were all young and healthy and could walk for miles without getting tired. None of the students had cars. Classes started about the first of September. I liked the teachers, and living conditions were better than at home, including the convenience of electricity.

6

Running Away from School

I wouldn't change most of the things I did when I was young. There is one exception, that being when I left school in Georgia and wandered around the country for about four years. I got friendly with a fellow I'll call Red because I don't remember his name. We talked about leaving school and going out west. I don't believe either of us would have gone anywhere alone. But we decided to go, and one morning while it was still dark we left school and started walking up the road. There wasn't much traffic. We walked until the middle of the day but still were only a few miles from where we had started, and we were hot and tired. Finally a car pulled over and stopped. The driver said, "Get in and keep your mouths shut." We got in the back, but there was no seat. It had been removed, and we were sitting on gallons of bootleg whiskey. They took off at full speed through the mountains around the little towns. Maybe they thought the law would be looking for two people and would be fooled because there were four of us. They finally got to where they were going and put us out. We were close to Asheville, and we caught another ride. We didn't know what to do or where to go.

We ended up in the railroad station, which stayed open all night at that time. There was no place to lie down, so we sat on the seats all night. The next morning we went out to the rail yards and caught a freight train headed west. We managed to get aboard, but they had seen us get on and at the next stop they made us get off. We spent the day in this little town. A couple of freight trains came through, but they didn't slow down. There was a revival service going on in a tent, and we walked over. They were getting started, and one man was the song leader. He kept trying to get the singers together, but they didn't seem to be listening. Finally he got really mad and hollered out, "I want all you damn singers down front!" We watched for a while but soon got bored and left. I had spotted a watermelon patch that afternoon, and I decided to try to get one. I got into the field, but about that time a light came on and somebody shouted, "Who's there?" I lay flat on the ground until everything got quiet. Then I sneaked away.

7

Learning to Be a Hobo

The next morning a freight train stopped at the water tank and we climbed aboard and rode to Knoxville. Lots of people were on the road that year. Some of them were World War I veterans who had been in Washington with the Bonus Marchers. They were traveling to get a bonus for their service during the war. They didn't sneak around. They went right into the rail yards and got off and on the boxcars whenever they wanted to. They were in their thirties and had beaten the Germans, and they were not about to let a railway detective push them around. Some even had their families with them. One of them showed me a poem he was writing. It started off, "Old Hoover said go home, boys, and dry up your tears. You won't get your bonus for twenty-one years."

I saw my first hobo jungle. A jungle was where some of the men would set up sort of a camp along the railroad, usually outside the city limits. Some cities would allow them to do this, but other places would sometimes break them up. They usually had someone who acted as a leader, and he would have them go into town to get something to eat. He might tell one person to get potatoes and another to get onions. They would send someone to a bakery to get old bread or buns. Sometimes the ones who went to the bakery might be put to work cleaning pots and pans, but they usually came back with something. The leader would pass the hat and get enough money to buy some meat to go in the stew.

Coffee was made in a gallon can. The water was brought to a boil, the coffee dropped in, and then it was taken off the fire. Some of the people had lived for years on the road. They liked to move around, and they wanted to be called hoboes, not bums. A hobo would work a while before moving on. The bums didn't travel and didn't want a job.

We spent the night at the jungle and met one of the people who was there. He was a sociable fellow and not much older than we were, but he had been on the road for a couple of years and we were impressed by his stories of travel around the country. We told him that we were headed west. He said that was where he was going and that he would help us get on the train. We had to get outside the yard, and the train would be picking up speed by the time it got to where we were waiting. I was carrying a suitcase, which would make it hard for me to catch the train. He told me that he could take the suitcase and give it back to me after we were aboard. We never saw him or the suitcase again. I had nothing but what I was wearing. My few dollars were still in the suitcase. We kept going. I knew there was no use trying to find him. He could have gone off in any direction.

We got to Chattanooga but kept on going. When we were a few miles out we came to a mountain. The train slowed down and a railroad detective started chasing everyone. I was hardheaded. He would make me get off and I would get back on again. He got tired of this foolishness, and the next time I got back on he caught me as I reached the top of the boxcar and stuck a pistol in my face. The barrel looked as big as a shotgun. This time I got down and stayed down. Several hours later another freight train came along and we got aboard and rode it into Nashville. I had not eaten for a couple of days, and I was getting desperate. I didn't want to beg, but I had to do something. The old hands told me that I needed to distance myself from the railroad, that the folks were tired of being hit up and they would probably sic the dogs on me or call the law, but I walked up to the first house I came to. I went to the back door and knocked. A lady came to the door, and I asked if she had some work I could do in exchange for food. She said I could move some wood from the yard and put it on the back porch. She was cooking on a wood stove. It wasn't much of a task, but it made me feel a little better. I don't know what would have happened if she had chased me away. I might have swallowed my pride and returned to the school or home. She cooked breakfast and fed me on the back porch. This perked me up and I continued on west to Memphis. I guess Red had enough of life on the road. I caught the train, but he didn't. I never heard from him again. I imagine he went back to North Georgia and stayed there.

I got to Memphis that night and went to the train station to have a place to spend the night. A man asked me where I was going, and I told him that I was traveling with no particular destination in mind. He then asked me if I wanted a ticket to a small town in western Kansas. He had bought a round-trip ticket and he wasn't going back. I took the ticket and got aboard the passenger train and rode it into Kansas City. This was a lot better than riding on the freight trains.

There was a layover of several hours before I could go the rest of the way. A man saw me and asked if I would help him load some watermelons on his truck. It didn't take long, but he gave me a dollar and I went to a café and had breakfast. I went back to the train station and used the remainder of the ticket. I believe the little town that I was going to was named Solomville. The last part of the trip was on a small electric train. I got off and looked around and decided to keep going, and for some reason or other I changed directions and headed south. I had meant to keep going west.

8

More Traveling and a Night in Jail

I hitchhiked to Wichita and then decided to ride a train from there. I was about to get on the train when a man called me. He didn't look like a cop. He was well dressed and very polite. He asked me where I was going. I told him I had been looking for work but didn't find any and was now headed home. I thought this was better than saying I was drifting around the country. He told me to get in the car, and when he stopped we were at the city jail. He told me I would have to stay a day or two. This was my first time being locked up. When the door clanged shut I realized that I was locked in, and it was not a good feeling. The man who had picked me up was the chief of police. At that time they could hold a prisoner as long as they wanted to and charge him with vagrancy. The object was to get your fingerprints and check to see if you were wanted anywhere for a crime. The jail was fairly clean, and the food was edible. I was told that I would be charged with breaking into the jail. A court was formed and a man presided as judge. There was a so-called lawyer for defense and a prosecutor. A jury was selected and I was asked how I would plead. I pleaded innocent to the charge. They found me guilty and fined me fifty cents, but they agreed to skip the fine because of my youth and ignorance and because I didn't have any money. This was what was called a kangaroo court. I don't know if they do anything like that anymore. I spent one day and night locked up and the second day they told me I could go, but the chief had a talk with me before I left. He said he wanted me to go home and go back to school and to write him a letter. I think his name was Wilson and that later on he became the chief of police in Chicago. I thought about writing him but never did. They released several prisoners at the same time they let me go. They hauled us to the city limits and told us to get going and not come back.

9

Learning about Life on the Road

I took their advice and headed south to Oklahoma. I went quite a way that day. That night, I arrived in a small town where a big circus was performing. I stood outside looking. Then I saw some workers moving things around. They didn't stop when entering the gate. I picked up a plank and passed on in with them. It was a good show, and I stayed until it was over. I was beginning to learn about life on the road. I found that you could usually take a bath at the Salvation Army. The hoboes called it the Sally, and if the workers had anything to eat they would feed you, although it might be cold oatmeal with blue-looking milk. They might lecture you a bit, but they were good people and still are. Gas station owners would let you use the rest rooms. People didn't mind picking up hitchhikers during those years. I found out that it was easier to catch a ride if you were alone. Some people would pick up one person but not two. After I learned that I avoided traveling with anyone when I was thumbing rides. I discovered that I could usually get something to eat if I would go in a decent place and ask the owner if he had any work that I could do in exchange for something to eat. You had to avoid looking like a bum, and you needed to speak up so that the people eating could hear you. It might make the owner mad, but he didn't want his customers to think he was a cheapskate. He would usually tell you to go in the kitchen and get something. Sometimes a customer would ask you to join him for a meal.

I left Oklahoma and hitchhiked to Fort Worth. I didn't stay there long. I decided to ride the freight trains and headed for El Paso. I got as far as Abilene when I started talking to a man and we got in the same boxcar. He had a big dog, and the dog jumped in, too. I had never seen anyone travel on freight trains with an animal, but he seemed to be managing all right. When the train got going we looked around and found that we were in a car that had been broken into. My companion turned pale and said if they caught us in there they would consider the case closed and we would probably do about two or three years on a Texas chain gang. There wasn't anything we could do at the moment. A couple of hours later the train came to a small town and we got off as soon as we could and started walking away. We headed across country. We wanted to get as far from the railroad as we could. We were headed toward Fort Stockton. Night caught us out in the middle of nowhere. We found an abandoned cabin and stopped for the night. There was a windmill pumping water in a trough. This was a watering place for the cattle, but there were no animals there, so we washed up. We had been without water most of the day, so we drank some of the water. It wasn't very good, but it helped quench our thirst. A large bird, a hawk, was at the watering trough and looked as though it had a broken wing. The man with me caught the bird and was going to try to do something for it, but the bird started pecking and clawing. He let the bird go, but not before he had a bloody hand.

We caught a ride into Fort Stockton and stopped at a combination gas station and café. Some Mexicans were eating lunch. They had been picking cotton and apparently had some money. One was wearing a white Stetson hat. A deputy sheriff walked in and for no apparent reason started beating the man over the head. The Mexican dropped the hat and ran. I don't think the sheriff had any reason to do this. He was just a bad character, and if anybody had tried to stop him he probably would have beaten him. When I got ready to leave I decided I didn't want to travel any farther with the man and his dog. I walked out to the edge of town and was picked up by a young couple. Chances are they wouldn't have stopped if I had still been with the man and his dog. This couple had some food in the car, and they shared it with me. They stopped a few miles out of El Paso. The man saw that my shoes were in bad shape, so he gave me a pair of his when I left the car. I saw an irrigation canal near the road, and I walked over and took a bath. I think the name of the place was Fabens. Most of the people were Mexicans, and it was some kind of a Mexican holiday. The people were dressed in their best outfits, and the bands were playing. It may have been Mexican Independence Day. Some of them shared food with me. It was the first time I had eaten Mexican food and I liked everything, but I really liked the tamales. I've never found any since then that tasted as good.

The next morning I caught a ride into El Paso and looked around for a while and then decided to cross over the bridge into Juarez. I was going to join a revolution if there was one going on, probably a result of reading too many bad magazines. I wasn't there long before I was approached by the police. They didn't speak much English, but I did understand they didn't want me in their country. They pointed at the bridge, and I crossed back over to El Paso.

10

Sudden Decision to Go Home

I suddenly decided to go home, although I had not thought much about it until then but after that I got in a hurry. I caught a train and headed east. I rode the same train for three days. I hardly took time to find anything to eat. One of the men on the train had money, and he invited me and one other fellow to eat with him when we got to Houston. I still remember what we ate. There was steak (the steak cost twenty-five cents), french fries, and sliced tomatoes. We finished eating and walked back to the railroad. We got there in time to catch the same train. A railway detective caught us and told us we were under arrest. The train started to move and I made a dive under the train and came out on the other side. It was a foolish thing to do and I could have been killed. I had heard about Houston, and they were supposed to have a place called the Pea Patch where they would work people on a farm, and sometimes they would hand out a ninety-day sentence. The detective let the others go when he was looking for me. All three of us got back on the train. The man who had bought the lunch really got on me for taking such a chance.

We continued on toward New Orleans. One time, for some reason, the train stopped out in the country by a sugarcane field. Everybody gathered the cane to chew on. It was all we had until we reached New Orleans. At that time there was no railway bridge into the city. The train had to be ferried across the Mississippi. I rode the ferry and reached New Orleans. I bought a poor boy sandwich for a nickel, and it was almost a meal. I hurried and soon reached the rail yards on the east side of town. I think the place was called Gentily. There were several people waiting to catch a ride. I sat down with some of the people who were waiting. It was almost dark, but I saw a man approaching and assumed that he was another transient. He was a railroad detective, and he had a big stick. It was about the size of a baseball bat. I was first in the line, and he hit me full force on the back. I don't know why it didn't cripple me. Most of the others got out of his way, and we moved farther out. The train would be moving pretty fast by the time it got to where we were waiting. Some thought it was too fast to hop on and didn't try it, but a few of us made it and rode east all night.

When we got to Atlanta we got off the train as soon as it slowed down. We didn't want to go into the yards because we knew the police might be waiting. You never knew when they would pick you up. Sometimes they didn't bother anyone, and at other times they might round up everyone coming in on the train. The bad thing about getting off the train at city limits was that you would have a long walk to get back to where you could hop on the train. If you had money, you could ride the streetcars. I didn't have a dime, and it was hard to hitchhike. I walked for miles and when night came I still had a long way to go. It was October and the nights were getting cold. I saw a house that appeared to be empty. I tried the door and it wasn't locked. The house was empty and I slept on the floor. The next day I walked to where I could get a train to take me the rest of the way. I was only about a hundred and fifty miles from home. I got to Anderson, South Carolina, about noon and was only about twelve miles from home. I had no idea what kind of reception I would get, but I imagined my parents would be very angry.

I had sent a few postcards home, but I hadn't heard anything from them. The first night, I stayed with a family that I knew. I cleaned up a little. I had not had a haircut for weeks and must have been pretty shaggy. A neighbor had a little barber-shop where he cut hair for a dime. I thought I'd have my haircut on credit, but he didn't charge me anything. I walked the final mile.

I think I felt like the prodigal son must have felt. As I approached the house my younger brothers and sisters spotted me and started yelling, "Here's Jack!" I had to face up to what I had done, and I knew that my mother was really disappointed with me. It was November before I started back to the local high school. I had to be in a grade behind the ones I had started out with. I still wanted to go places and see things.

*   *   *

Part III

11

Trying to Get a Job in Florida

A man in our little town was hauling oranges from Florida, and he gave me a ride in the back of his truck to Lakeland, Florida. I hitchhiked to Tampa and tried to get a job on a boat. Even the people who had seaman's papers were having a hard time getting jobs. I went to a small town called Palm Harbor. *My mother's first cousin was in business there. He had been a poor farmer in North Georgia, but he lost an arm in an accident and decided he had to do some other kind of job. He bought a truck and he and his boys went to Florida to work in the orange groves. The boys picked fruit and he drove the truck. He did so well that he moved his family to Florida. He expanded operations, and when I got there he had several trucks and was managing crews that were picking fruit. He had not done well when he had two arms but was doing well with just one arm. He had a big house and a large family of children and grandchildren.* I stayed a couple of weeks and helped out around the place but still had time to look around. Florida was a nice place to live or visit at that time and was not crowded.

12

Return Home to Help on the Farm

I returned home in the spring and decided to help grow a crop. They needed me because my two older brothers had left home. Another brother would also help. We would take care of the work on the home place, and he and I would get a few acres to work on the halves. That is called share-cropping. The owner furnished the mules and equipment and also the fertilizer. The crop was divided evenly. My father would get half, and my brother and I would get one-fourth each. The younger brothers would help with the hoeing and picking cotton. We made a good crop, but we got about thirty dollars a bale and we ended up with about thirty dollars each for our part. I decided then that I was finished with farming.

The year was 1933 and the country was still in a deep depression. Roosevelt had been sworn in as president, but most of his programs had not gotten very far. Later there would be the WPA (Works Progress Administration) and the CCC (Civilian Conservation Corps). I didn't go back to school in the fall. I helped pull corn. You needed to have enough to last a year. You needed it to feed the mules, hogs, and chickens. We ate cornbread at noon and night. The crop that year was average. After frost we went to the field and pulled the crop. We pulled the corn and piled it on the ground. Then we got the mules hooked up to the wagon and hauled the corn to the barn and unloaded. Before we brought in the new crop we would clean out what was left of the last year's crop. When we got to the bottom of the old crop the rats would start coming out and running all over the place. We would have the dogs standing by, and each one of us would have a big stick. We killed a lot of rats, but never got them all.

When we got through with the corn I helped pull corn for an old man who lived next door. His boys were grown and had moved away. He paid me fifty cents a day. It wasn't much, but I was glad to earn anything. We went to the woods to get the next year's supply of wood for the wood stove. It had to have time to cure out before we used it. After we cut the trees we would load them into the wagon, take them home, and cut the wood into the right lengths for the stove. If the trees had been cut at the wrong time of the moon the wood would not cure out as it should and wouldn't make a good fire.

There was plenty of time for loafing in the winter. Since there was no electricity we read by a kerosene lamp and we sat by the fire in the evenings. There was lots of visiting. People used to say, "Come over to the house and sit until bedtime." The old folks would tell stories, and sometime they would pop corn in the fireplace. There were little country stores all around the neighborhoods. When the work was done people would go to a store and play checkers and catch up on the local news. Most of the country stores had corn mills. They would grind up corn for meal and grits.

The hunting season opened on Thanksgiving, and everybody would hunt once or twice a week. There wasn't any big game, but people who owned dogs liked to run them. Most of the time they brought home a few rabbits. We had rabbit dogs, but the folks had picked up a collie somewhere and she was the best squirrel dog I ever saw. She would tree them. They were not very big and they were hard to skin, but my mother cooked them with dumplings and they were better than chicken.

13

Leaving Home Again to Find a Job

A few days after the holidays I left home and went to Charleston to try to get work on a ship. In order to get a job you needed to belong to the union and you needed to have experience. I met a couple of men who were trying to get a ship. They were staying in a place that let sailors stay for a few days while they looked for a ship. They came up with an idea, and somehow or other they fixed me up with papers that showed me to be an able-bodied seaman. This was a grade higher than an ordinary seaman, which is what you start out with. I moved into the seamen's home where I had bed and board while I looked for a ship. This didn't cost me anything, but I had to move out after a week. There were no jobs for anyone at that time. I enjoyed my stay, though, and spent a lot of time looking around the place. We were running out of time in the home, and my friends were going to Wilmington, North Carolina, to try their luck there. We rode a freight train to Columbia and got there at night. At that time there was a big market on Market Street that stayed open all night and people built fires to keep warm. We spent the night there, and the next day we headed for Wilmington. We couldn't find a direct connection by train, so we started to hitchhike in that direction. I was doubtful that someone would pick up three people, but a truck that had been hauling fertilizer stopped and picked us up. We rode in the back, and it was a rough ride.

We got to Wilmington before night and checked in the seamen's home that night. The next day we started trying to get a job on a ship. Somebody must have told us about a ship that was anchored in the river. We got a boat to take us out to the ship. We went aboard, and the other men knew some of the crew. There were no jobs available, but I had the opportunity to ride on a launch. I decided to give up the idea of going to sea.

The next morning I headed north by myself. I got to Richmond, Virginia. The second day there was some kind of government program for hiring the unemployed. The pay wasn't much, but they had a place for transients to stay and there were a couple of meals included. The work assignment I had was to remove some wooden blocks from an old bridge. I worked one day and also went to the job the following day. The bridge was over a railroad track, and I could hear a train in the distance. It was spring and I had the urge to travel, so I picked up what little gear I had and climbed down to the tracks. The train came through, and I caught it. We were headed west and we passed through some mountains. I was riding on top of the train and I looked just in time as we entered a tunnel. It was black as midnight, and the smoke and cinders got all over me. I wasn't in a hurry, and I stopped in some of the little West Virginia towns. They were coal-mining towns, and the people were friendly. It was still a little cold at night, and sometimes I would ride the train at night and find a place to sleep in the daytime. Nobody bothered me, and most of the time I would be the only person on the train except the crew. When we got to Charleston, West Virginia, it was different. They were rounding up people and putting them in jail. They might have been on the lookout for an escaped criminal. They fingerprinted everyone and held them in jail for a couple of days, which gave the police time to get a report back on the fingerprints. On Monday morning they let us go and I continued on my way to Ohio. We pulled into a rail yard. It was cold and I didn't see any place to get warm. One of the men with us had worked on the railroad, and he saw an engine idling in the yard. A couple of us went with him, and we climbed up in the cab of the engine. We stayed warm and no one bothered us. The next day I crossed the river and was in Ohio. I caught a train north. It wasn't cold, but it snowed most of the way. You could see green grain sticking up through the snow. I spent one more day on the road.

14

Visiting My Brother in Ohio and Going to Work

My brother Charlie had left home a couple of years before I did, but he didn't leave in the manner that I did. He had rented some land and planted cotton. It happened to be a good year, and he made enough to get some clothes and train fare. He knew a man from home who was working in a dime store in Youngstown, Ohio, and got a job there. They paid low wages and worked their people long hours, but Charlie didn't complain. He was glad to be through farming.

When I got to Youngstown, Ohio, I found my brother's home right away, and I was there when he got home from his job. He was surprised to see me, as no one had told him that I was coming. In fact, when I left home I had not decided where I would go.

I started looking for work, but there didn't seem to be anything for me. One day I took a bus to the better part of town. When I got there I knocked on the door of the biggest house on the block. A lady came to the door, and I asked if she had any work for me to do around the yard. She invited me in and told me that her husband had a plant just outside the city limits and he was going to hire a few people. She gave me the address and a note to take to her husband. I went to the plant and tried to get in the gate where they were hiring. The place was lined up with men who had heard about possible jobs. The line didn't seem to be moving, and

I went around to the back and climbed over the fence. I got to the office, but the lady must have called about me, because I was not interviewed, but they just told me to report the next morning. I had never worked in a factory, but it wasn't hard. The pay was about four dollars per day. People at home were working at jobs that paid less. In fact, it was more than my brother was making in the dime store. I bought a pass to ride a bus for a dollar a week. You could get a transfer and go all over town. On weekends, I would ride out to a park and take walks, and there was an amusement park that had rides, a swimming pool, and bingo. My brother moonlighted by working at the bingo games. I wanted people to know I had a job, so for a while I would wear work clothes home. Most of the men cleaned up before leaving the job. The plant was called the Youngstown Steel Door Manufactury and they were building doors for boxcars. After I had been there a couple of months they cut back production and I was laid off. They said they would call us back later if they needed help. I didn't leave an address where I could be contacted. I knew I wasn't coming back. I had bought some clothes and still had some money.

* * *

Part IV

15

1934–37, Traveling and Selling Magazine Subscriptions

Just before leaving Youngstown, Ohio, I saw an ad in the newspaper about a job for young men eighteen to twenty to travel the USA. Interviews were being held at the Todd House Hotel, probably the best hotel in town at that time. I wore my best clothes and was hired right away. They were hiring anyone who was halfway presentable. There was no salary and the only pay would be part of the money received from selling subscriptions to magazines. I was sent out with one of the crew members to teach me the routine. The sales talk was called a spiel. The man who trained me was a Mr. Johnson from Iowa, and he had been with the group for several months. I recall that the date was June 6, 1934. The spiel was presented in different ways, but the idea was that you were a poor boy working your way through college receiving points for each subscription or renewal. Sometimes you would be an orphan living with an aunt. Mr. Johnson made a few sales that day, but some didn't buy his story.

We had most of the current magazines. Prices ranged from the twenty-five-cent *Needle Craft* to the eight-dollar *Vogue.* Our quota was eight dollars in subscriptions per day, and we kept one-half. Out of that we had to pay for our meals, rooms, and laundry. Most of the rooms cost one dollar, or we could share a room and pay fifty cents each. Later on we stayed in tourist cabins that had central baths and were usually situated in a grove of trees. In the summer I preferred the cabins to hotels; this was before they had motels. The cabins rented for fifty cents per night, and most of them were clean and comfortable. Meals were usually not more than twenty-five cents. If we made our quota we would have twenty-four dollars. At that time that was more than most workers were earning, especially in the South. After a couple of weeks I was making enough to get by. We worked around Youngstown for a few days and then went to Pennsylvania. Each morning we would go into a town and start working. Usually we were dropped off a few miles out from the center of town and would work our way back, meeting at the post office in the afternoon. The next day we moved to another town and started over. There were generally six to eight crews working for one man. I went with a different crew each week. We were working for the National Circulations Company, located at Rockefeller Center in New York City. On Saturday nights we got what money we had left and spent it all that night.

We moved into the New England states. It was summer and the weather was nice. New Englanders were readers and it was easy to make our quota and sometimes more. One of the men in the crew was called Jew Williams. I don't believe he was Jewish, and I doubt that was his name. We could call ourselves anything we wanted to, but I kept my name the whole time. Some who had foreign-sounding names changed to something that sounded American.

One day I had a chance to see Williams operate. We left the station wagon and walked a short distance before selecting a house. He finally picked a large house in a good neighborhood, and we rang the bell. The lady invited us in, and he started his story. He asked the lady if she had read about the accident that happened last Easter Sunday in a nearby town in which two people were killed. She said that she did remember and in fact had read about it at that time. He told her that was his mother and father. He said that when it happened he had been in college, but he had been forced to drop out because of a lack of funds. He told her that by completing the current contest he would be able to return to college the next semester. By this time he and the lady of the house were both crying. I excused myself and left the house. I knew that I could not put on a performance like that and would not even if I could. I didn't mind a few stories, but this was too much. It was strange what some of the crew got away with. Sometimes one of them would tell the lady of the house that at one time he was her paperboy and the lady would say she thought she remembered. Naturally she would want to do him a favor by taking a subscription. We worked in all of the New England states most of the summer and were there until Thanksgiving.

For a few days in August we had crossed over into Montreal, Canada, but we didn't try to sell magazine subscriptions there, as it would have been illegal without special permission. We liked Canada, although most of the people spoke French. There were places to see, and some of us went for a ride in a horse-drawn vehicle. We were at a place called the Plains of Abraham. The food was good and inexpensive. The girls were mostly of French descent and quite friendly. Most of them spoke some English. We regretted having to return to work in the United States. After Thanksgiving we crossed over the Hudson River into Newberg, New York.

After we left New York State we started south. We traveled down Highway #11 from Pennsylvania. It was fall and the weather was still warm most of the time. We could usually make our quota without too much difficulty in the Shenandoah Valley, but when we got further south it was hard to sell enough to average eight dollars a day in sales. Most of the folks didn't read the kind of magazines we had been selling. Now we would try to sell true-story magazines or something that cost a dollar or less. But they were polite, and no one had a door slammed in his face. That had happened in the North sometimes, especially if you came across someone who had been cheated. Things were misrepresented at times, but we always sent the magazine subscriptions people had purchased.

16

Quick Visit with My Family and Then Heading West

We reached my hometown of Anderson, South Carolina. The crew checked in the local hotel and began working there and in the surrounding communities. I didn't work but I stayed with my folks until we were ready to move on. One night my folks had the eight-man crew at our home for a wonderful homemade meal. They even had a fire going in the parlor, and everyone enjoyed the evening. Some of the men told me I would be better off if I stayed home. I still wanted to travel, though, especially since we were headed for the West Coast.

After we started west we moved faster. The plan was to meet the other crews and spend Christmas in Los Angeles. We stopped in New Orleans the first weekend and stayed in Mont Leone Hotel. It was in the center of all the activities. We went sightseeing and stopped at the Absinthe House, where the doors stayed open around-the-clock back then. At midnight we were on a boat and cruised down the river and back. New Orleans was a fun town.

We headed west the following Monday and made it to El Paso, Texas, for the next weekend. We had to sell magazines, but we had to go several hundred miles. We liked El Paso and crossed over the border to eat supper on Saturday night. Monday morning we started west. We spent a lot of time on the road but still managed to sell enough to keep up our quota of eight dollars per day, of which we got 50 or 60 percent of the sales.

17

California

On the following Sunday we arrived at the town of Indior, California. It was almost midnight when we got there, and we checked in at the first hotel we came to. The night manager asked if we wanted a room with or without a woman. We had traveled several hundred miles that day, and we told him we wouldn't be interested in having a woman for the night. I never saw any of the women, and apparently they had gone home for the night. We left in the morning and started selling magazine subscriptions. I kept seeing signs about date milkshakes. I bought one but thought it was too sweet. This was the only place I ever saw date palms.

Late in the afternoon we arrived at Palm Springs. At that time the town was still small but very attractive in winter. There were some movie stars around, but I didn't see them. Will Rogers and Joan Crawford were supposed to be in town.

I was allowed to use the station wagon the next day and worked out of town and had the opportunity to see the Kellogg family. I think they were the people who made cornflakes. I had an easy day and sold about double the quota of eight dollars per day. I've been back to Palm Springs a few times, but it had changed from the place it had been in 1935.

The next day we crossed over the mountains to Laguna Beach. It was still a small town but very attractive. We sold subscriptions there and in some of the small towns along the coast.

On Saturday we worked most of the day, but late in the afternoon we drove into Los Angeles. It was a couple of days before Christmas. We checked into a hotel and joined some of the people from the other crews. We had a good time and saw Hollywood and surrounding areas. One day I visited a cousin and his wife who were living in Los Angeles. He was a drifter and had lived in many parts of the country.

One day most of the crew decided to go to Santa Catalina. We left the hotel early in the morning, drove to the beach, and got the ship. It was a nice trip and gambling was legal on the ship. I won the jackpot on a slot machine. It was only a few dollars, but at that time it seemed really big. We got to the island and went out on a glass-bottom boat. The water was clear and we could see lots of fish. When we returned to shore we heard that Zane Grey had a house there. We had read some of his books, and we took off up the hill to his house. He wasn't there, but a couple of ladies invited us in and showed us around. *Later when I was in New Zealand I visited a house that he had stayed in while there. I never did get to meet him, and later on I lost interest in most of his books.*

One of the men had a brother stationed on a naval ship that was in San Diego. We drove down for the day and he must have been expecting us, because he met us on the dock and carried us out to his ship. It was a destroyer and we had to walk across a couple of ships to reach it. Everything was quiet and I suppose that most of the crew must have been on Christmas leave. He showed us around the ship, and we stayed and had lunch. I didn't have any interest in joining the service at that time. We looked around downtown San Diego, but there didn't seem to be much going on. Many of the buildings were closed.

We went back to Los Angeles and spent the night. The next day we left and went back to work selling magazine subscriptions.

We worked our way up the coast and stopped at Santa Barbara. It was a nice, quiet town at that time, and most of the people were retired. We spent one night there, and the next morning we drove inland a few miles. We spread out around the town, but in a very short time we were picked up one by one and put in jail. They called it the Green River Law. It was named for the town of Green River, Wyoming. According to this law, you were trespassing if you approached a house without an invitation and tried to sell something. The police chief was really glad to pick us up. He didn't have anybody else in his jail, and he made a big deal about arresting us. I heard him telling his wife or someone else on the phone that he was too busy to talk to her because he was tied up with important work. He was taking fingerprints and asking questions. I guess our crew chief had a telephone number he could call, because we were let go after a couple of hours. I don't know if there is still a Green River Law or not.

We worked our way north and ended up in Sacramento for the weekend. The following Monday we started out to the small towns in the area. I don't remember why I was crew chief that week, but I ended up driving the station wagon and managing the crew. There was no extra pay for the crew chief, but you could use the car and get in areas that you couldn't reach on foot. Also, there was prestige in arriving by vehicle. We worked all that week in the old gold-mining towns. Some were still operating. The ones that had closed usually had some prospectors out panning in the creeks. The first day I picked up one of the men. He had not sold a thing, but he said he wanted to work the same place again in the afternoon. I knew what he was up to. He had spent the morning with a woman and had not been trying to sell subscriptions. I didn't argue with him, but I just told him that he would have to come with us or he could get back to the hotel on his own and that if he didn't start selling something he would be fired when we got back to the hotel. He worked in the afternoon and reached his quota for the day.

We enjoyed working the old mining towns. Most of them had been famous in their day. The price of gold at that time was only about thirty-six dollars an ounce. Later when the price went up some of the old mines reopened. It was a nice part of the country at that time. I suppose by now it is completely different.

18

Oregon, Washington, Idaho, Nevada, Utah, Colorado, South Dakota, Iowa, and Illinois

We moved on up to Oregon the following week. We worked our way up, passing through the small towns and ending up in Portland for the weekend. We all made our quota. That part of the country had not suffered as much from the depression as the South and East.

We traveled up the coast, working the towns along the way. We spent one week around Tacoma. It was a nice town and was more prosperous than most of the country. We spent a few days in the old wooden hotel. I think the name was the Tacoma. It burned down a few years later, but at that time it was a very nice place. They were making a movie about Alaska. Some of the actors were staying in the hotel. Clark Gable and Jack Oakie were supposed to be there, but I didn't see them.

One day as I was working in the city I stopped at a house to try to make a sale. I didn't know who the people were but found out later they were the Weyhousers, owners of a lumber company by that same name. They didn't seem very different from their neighbors. The lady of the house introduced me to her family. One of the boys was kidnapped later. I don't remember the details, but I believe he was returned to his family. She bought a couple of subscriptions, and I did not know who the family was until later when I read about them in the newspapers.

We worked most of the small towns around Seattle and Tacoma and spent the weekend in Seattle. The following week we worked north of Seattle all the way to the Canadian border. It was a nice part of the state, and we had a good week and were back in Seattle the following week.

The next week we started east, working the small towns along the way. I had a distant relative in a town called Rosylyn. I asked about him and was directed to an old house on the edge of town. *He had left South Carolina many years before and didn't come back for a long time. Before he left he had borrowed a railroad locomotive engine that was parked in Belton, South Carolina, and had driven it a few miles and left it. He had not damaged anything, but he wasn't taking any chances. The next time we heard from him he was in a small town in Nevada. He had the gold fever, and when I saw him he had been working a claim near where he was living. He wasn't very prosperous and I don't think he ever had much success, but I guess he had been doing what he wanted to do.* He asked me not to tell his folks back east that he wasn't doing very well. He had been back only once in over forty years. I gave him a few dollars, and I could tell that he wanted me to leave so he could go to the nearest bar. *A few years later when I was back east I heard that he had been killed in a pool room. Someone had hit him with a cue stick.*

Washington State is an attractive place, and we covered most of it. I liked the names of the towns. We were in Yakima, Wenatchee, Omak, Okanogan, and Kettle Falls. There were many more places, but I thought the towns along the Columbia River were the prettiest. This part of the country was better off than most of the United States. I talked to one woman who had a large apple orchard. She said that she and her husband had been trying to make it farming in

Nebraska and had decided to relocate. Several years ago they had rented a boxcar from the railroad and loaded up what little property they had, including a cow, and moved to Washington State. She didn't say how they had accomplished it, but when I met them they were quite successful. They subscribed to several magazines and wished me good luck.

We made it to Spokane for the weekend. Then we worked our way south and made it to Boise, Idaho, for the next weekend. We got to Nevada and spent one weekend in Reno. (*Several years ago I returned to Reno to attend a reunion of the Marine battalion that I had served with in World War II. At that time it was still small, but it was a wide open place and much smaller than it is now.*)

It was winter and snow was on the ground, but the humidity was low and it didn't feel cold. We kept working our way back east. After leaving Utah we worked western Colorado, ending up at the Brown Hotel in Denver on a weekend. About the end of March we had passed through the Black Hills of South Dakota and were in Iowa. It was spring, but the weather was wet and cold most of the time. Iowa at that time was one of the best states to sell magazine subscriptions. The farms were spread out, and in the winter there was not a whole lot to do, just routine farm chores. Later on when they started getting ready to plant the corn they would be working long hours. Most of the small towns had a large Catholic church where we could sell to the local priests. We spent about a month working Iowa, and later we worked in Illinois. When we got to Chicago I decided to take some time off.

19

Time off in Hot Springs, Arkansas, Then to Tennessee, Massachusetts, Maine, and New York City

I had been feeling some stiffness when working out in the cold, and I decided to go to Hot Springs, Arkansas, to bathe in the spas. I think I heard about the place from one of the men in our crew who was from a small town near Hot Springs. I left Chicago on a Saturday afternoon and decided to save some money by hopping a freight train, although it had been a good while since I had done this. I wore my oldest clothes and carried a small bag. I took a streetcar out to the rail yards and caught the next freight train south. It was fast and did not stop often. I didn't find any open box-cars, so I had to ride on top of one. I got very sleepy later on and I was afraid of going to sleep and falling off. I took my belt and secured myself to the catwalk and went to sleep. Early the next morning I arrived in Memphis, Tennessee. I went to a café to get breakfast. I had some dirt and black smoke on my face, so I used the rest room to clean up and change clothes. The waitress helped me get a cinder out of my eye. I then ordered breakfast and rested a while before continuing on my way. Since I had cleaned up I decided to finish the trip by hitchhiking. It was easy to get rides, but most of the people who picked me up were only going a short way. Even so, I arrived at my destination before night. I started taking the hot baths. By that time I was feeling better, but I continued taking the baths. I bathed and exercised in the mornings and in the afternoons hiked on the nearby trails. It was spring of the year, and the dogwood trees were blooming. A man who had worked with us lived in town a few miles away. I let him know where I was, and he came and spent a day visiting.

Hitchhike to Boston

I knew where the magazine crew was supposed to be, and I started hitchhiking to Boston to catch up with them. I made good time on the road until I crossed into Massachusetts. It was late and I caught a ride that left me off out in the country. It was getting dark and I didn't think I would get a ride, so I got off the road and spent the night in some woods. I had a good night's sleep and the next morning caught rides and got to Boston before night. I found the hotel where the crew was staying. It was Saturday night, and I joined up with some of them and started seeing the town. We ended up in a bar that had silver dollars embedded in the bar, and one of the men tried to pick them up—without success of course.

Monday morning I was back working with the crew. We traveled every week and once we got as far as Bar Harbor, Maine. At one small town we were approached by a group of officers who put on their sirens and halted us. They approached our station wagon with pistols drawn. They ordered us out of our vehicle and lined us up by the side of the road. We had leather cases for our subscription blanks, and I suppose they looked like holsters for pistols. After checking us out the officers let us go. It seems there had been some gangs operating around the country who were dangerous.

We covered all the New England states. On the weekend of the Fourth of July we were out near the end of Long Island. I think the name of the place where we stayed was Shelter Island. The ocean water was cold, but we swam anyway. After the holiday weekend we started working some of the estates along the way. Some of our men did well at these fine homes. I made some sales, but it was hard to get to talk to the people who owned these big estates. Some had guardhouses out by the road, and we couldn't see the owners. I was not doing very well, so I quit and hitchhiked into New York City. We were supposed to arrive there on Saturday afternoon. The first night, I rode the subways. The next morning, I got some breakfast at an automat and then went to the RKO building, which was where the circulation company was located. I told them that I was quitting and started to turn in my blank subscriptions. They were fine people. They urged me to stay until the rest of the crew got into town for the weekend. They seemed happy to meet someone who had sold subscriptions all across the country. They told me where my crew would be staying for the weekend, so I went there and checked in. Our men arrived on Saturday afternoon. They had not made a lot of sales, and no one seemed mad at me for leaving in the middle of the week. That night, we went out on the town. We were told that we should be all right, but it would not be wise to go to Harlem. About half a dozen of our men did go there and were robbed. Luckily, no one was hurt. On Sunday we went out to the beaches, but it was crowded and hot. We went on some of the rides and ate hot dogs. On Monday morning we spread out in all directions and went to work giving our spiels. I worked a couple of weeks and then decided I needed a change.

20

Visit My Folks and Pick up a Traveling Companion—Alabama, Oklahoma, Texas, and Colorado

I left the crew and hitchhiked to South Carolina, but after a few weeks I was ready to go back on the road. A fellow I knew wanted to go with me. I usually traveled alone, but I let him talk me into taking him along. He had relatives living in Birmingham, Alabama. We rode freight trains and did all right until we got to Alabama. We were picked up by a couple of mean railroad detectives. One of them wanted an excuse to beat us up. He cursed us and called us all kinds of names. He wanted us to try something and give him an excuse to use his club on us. We stood there and said nothing. Finally he let us go. We stopped to visit my friend's relatives. I didn't think they would be happy to have a couple of bums visit them, but they seemed glad to have us for a visit and we stayed a couple of days.

After that we decided to hitchhike and had good luck. We made it to Oklahoma in two days. A man who gave us a ride was listening to his radio, and the news came on about Will Rogers getting killed in an airplane crash in Alaska. He was very popular and in Oklahoma it was almost like losing one of the family. We traveled on to Amarillo, Texas, and arrived late. It was dark and people didn't like picking up hitchhikers at night, so we went to the rail yards and caught a freight train into Colorado. We stopped in Denver and washed up at a filling station. Most station owners would let us use their rest rooms to clean up if they were not busy. We got some breakfast at the Salvation Army. It wasn't anything fancy, but a little oatmeal and coffee tasted good in the mornings. We didn't stay very long in Denver.

We caught a freight train heading west, and the next morning we were up at ten-thousand-feet elevation. It felt cold, although it was summertime. I washed my face in a stream, and it was refreshing. We crossed over the Rockies and got to Delta, Colorado. The people I planned to visit had a farm a few miles out of town. I had not met any of the family except Doyle Wilson, who had been on the magazine crew with us back east. We stayed a few days and then got ready to continue on my trip. My traveling companion decided he had gone far enough, and we parted as friends. I don't believe he ever made any more trips.

21

Alone Again, Heading West—a Job in Utah, Reno, and Sacramento

After that I headed west and stopped in Green River, Utah, and got a job hoeing cantaloupes. I had been there a year before and had worked picking melons. It was early in the season, but they needed some workers. We were not pushed for time, and I was able to get weekends off. One man I had picked melons with was still there. He had gotten permission to open up an old coal mine and was making enough income to feed his large family. The two oldest boys were helping in the coal mine. It was a simple operation. They dug in on the side of a hill and didn't have any special equipment. I doubt if you could operate like that now. They kept a horse on the farm, and they let me ride it. I would ride to the little town of Green River or go the other direction along the river to the north. (*About fifty years later my wife and I were touring the west and when we reached Green River we drove to where I had worked many years before. We found the place where I had worked, but everything had changed. No one was farming. I asked questions and was told they had stopped farming because no one wanted to do that kind of work anymore, but I think the soil had become too alkaline.*)

I worked for a few weeks and I got a ride with an old couple who were driving to the west coast for a college reunion. He was one of the prominent citizens and a big land owner in the little town of Green River. He did all the driving and made good time. We reached Reno the second day and spent the night there. After we got rooms I went out to the night spots and started playing blackjack. A man was playing and he asked me if I was on the road. I told him that I was and he said I would be better off if I didn't gamble. Then he told me he was working there as a shill. A shill uses the club's chips, and it is his job to keep the game going. I took his advice and just looked around and kept the money I had earned working in the cantaloupe fields.

The next day we reached Sacramento and I left them and looked up a man I had worked with back east while selling magazine subscriptions. He had married, but they had split up before I got there. He invited me to stop over for a few days, but he was living with his father, who did not want any company. I spent the night, but the next day I headed north.

22

Mining in California

I caught a ride with a man, and he turned off the main road in Siskyoo County. I went along with him. We stopped in a small town, and when he left I stayed there. It was an old town, and there wasn't much going on. People had found gold in the area years before, and one mine was still operating when I got there. I stayed at an old inn, a place without very many guests. There were a few old-timers living there. The next morning I talked with some of the local people and they told me that someone had opened an old mine nearby and was hiring some help. I got my bag and caught a ride to the mine. I talked with a clerk and he told me if I wanted a job I could go to work the next day. I reported to the bunkhouse and was assigned a place to sleep. I had my meals at the mess hall, and they had good food. It wasn't fancy, but there was plenty, and the cooks did a good job serving about fifty people. After we ate we prepared to go into the mine. I had my miner's cap with the little carbide light. We entered from the side of the hill and followed a horse-drawn mining cart. It was slightly uphill to the end of the tunnel where we were digging. The horse was then unhitched and taken back to the entrance of the mine. The horse wasn't needed in returning the cart. In fact, someone had to return the cart to the outside of the mine and use the brake on the way out. One of the experienced miners placed the dynamite in holes that were drilled in the rocks.

He would place the dynamite, and we would go back a distance and wait for the blast; then we would return and fill the cart with the debris. The cart would be unloaded outside the mine, and then the horse would pull the cart back to where we were waiting. It was not hard work and at the time I was not overly concerned about the danger. After about three weeks they started laying off some of the workers and I was one of the people let go. This didn't bother me, as I was planning to move on anyway.

23

Celebrate My Twenty-First Birthday, July 6, 1936, with Two New Mining Friends

I had met a couple of people who were higher up the mountains. One was working sluice boxes in the creek. Another was higher up and had sunk shafts in the hillside. He was a hard-rock miner and had invested more into his operation. He could work all year round. He had built a log cabin, and he had running water in his kitchen. He had located a spring a short way above his place, and the water was piped into his kitchen. I don't believe he ever cut the water off, just let it overflow and run out the back of his cabin. His name was Robinson and I believe he had mined just about all of his life. This was in 1936. (*In 1946 my wife and I were on vacation from Camp Pendleton, California, and we climbed up to his place. It had been ten years since I had heard anything about these people. He remembered me and was very happy to meet my wife. He let her use his kitchen. It was plain fare, but after the walk up the mountains we were hungry. He told me that he had gone to Utah and had panned for gold in the Colorado River. He said he had found some gold but decided to return to his place in California. It must have been lonely for him in the winter. I don't think he could have gotten in and out during the coldest months, but he could work in the mine.*)

The other man on the stream was below Robinson. He was at a lower elevation and could drive to his place. He was a Frenchman named Bougeau. *He had been an officer in World*

War I. He had tried to get in the movies in Hollywood. I think he might have had some small parts but had not managed to make a career there. He had an old house on his place, but he had built a small cabin and was living in it. I guess it was easier to keep warm in the smaller place. He said that I could move into the old house and help in his operation. I went back to the bunkhouse and got my luggage and moved into the old house. I ate at his place, which was not far from where I was staying. He was a good cook and I had my meals at his house, but I always returned to my house after I finished eating. I would join him at the sluice boxes on the creek during the day. His operation was not like his neighbor's, and I don't believe he could do anything in the winter. At this elevation the stream would be frozen over for several months. I was there on my birthday, July 6, 1936. He made a cake and Mr. Robinson came down from his place. I was twenty-one years old, and they congratulated me and said they wished they were twenty-one again. After about a month I got the urge to move on. We parted friends, and Bougeau gave me a piece of quartz that had a streak of gold in it. I sold it later to a Chinese man for a few dollars. I got a ride into the next little town. I had bought a few work clothes on credit at the little store. I paid them and then started hitchhiking north.

24

Hitchhiking North

I was near the Oregon border when I stopped at the first town. People were panning for gold in a stream. I don't know if they were finding enough to make it pay, but it was better than doing nothing. There was a small hotel in the little town. I went in for lunch, and when I finished eating the woman who owned the place came to my table. She asked if I had ever worked as a waiter, and I told her I had not. She said she thought that I would be good at the job. I wasn't looking for a job but decided to give it a try. She assigned me to a room and told me I could go to work the next morning. I reported early the next day, but I didn't like waiting on tables. One of the staff seemed to be going with the owner, and he recommended that I be put to work in the kitchen. I started washing dishes. They called it pearl diving. It wasn't bad and I liked the workers. They drank a lot of cheap wine and seemed to enjoy their work. I cleared the plates before putting them in the washer. I was told not to throw away food. If anything was left and had not been partially eaten I was to set it aside, and it would be served again. Scraps might be used in making soups. It probably would not have been approved by the state board of health, but at that time people were struggling to stay in business.

25

On the Road Again with the Old Sales Crew, Home for the Holidays, and New Job

I stayed a few days and then left for Portland, Oregon. I read an ad in the paper about hiring young men to travel and sell magazines, and I knew that was one of the crews I had worked with before. I caught a ride into Portland and went to the hotel where the magazine crew was staying. There were two brothers with the first names of Paul and Silas who were running the crews. They were from a small town in North Carolina and had done well in the business. Each one had a station wagon to haul the crews. I had not worked for them, but I knew some of the people with them. They told me to move into the hotel and go to work the following Monday. I worked with them until we got back east.

I left my work companions about a week before Christmas 1936 and started hitchhiking, but I only caught short rides. I had planned on being home for the holidays, but on Christmas Eve I was still about two hundred miles from home and it began to get dark. I quit trying to get rides and stopped at a little town south of Atlanta, Georgia. I got a room in the boardinghouse and the next morning was back on the road, managing to reach home before dark. My folks were glad to see me, and I stayed until the New Year.

I had been selling magazines for more than two years and was starting to think about doing something else. I saw an ad for young men to travel and found out the manager would be in a nearby town the first week in January. He wanted me to start right away. He was married and his wife was with him. He had one man and two girls working for him. Both girls were nice-looking and usually managed to do well in selling magazine subscriptions. We headed north and I was able to make my usual average.

26

Make a Life-changing Decision

When we got to Virginia I was working just a short distance from the capital. I called at a home and was invited in by a man who was a recently retired marine officer. He showed me his collection of items brought from China. *I think his last tour of duty had been in Peking. I don't believe he had wanted to leave the service, but at that time promotions were extremely slow and if you were passed over a couple of times you were probably at the end of your career. It was different for the enlisted personnel. Some of them stayed for more than thirty years.* I was interested in hearing about the Marine Corps, but I had not planned on enlisting in any of the military services.

We left Washington, D.C., and headed for Baltimore. After working all day I was supposed to be picked up at the main post office, but it was late and I missed the crew. I got a room for the night and headed back to the post office the next morning. I thought they would be there waiting for me, but they were late.

I started looking around and saw a large Marine Corps recruiting sign. There was a picture of a marine in khakis wearing his campaign hat. He was on a tropical island with palm trees and was using semaphore flags to communicate with a destroyer offshore. In the picture the sun was shining and flowers were blooming. In Baltimore it was cloudy and dismal. I wasn't convinced that I was interested in military service, but my crew still had not arrived, so I decided to kill time by talking to the marine recruiter. He was a fine-looking person and was wearing a dress blue uniform with chevrons and campaign ribbons. He also was wearing his expert rifle badge. He greeted me as if I were an old friend. I don't remember all that was said, but about an hour later I was sworn in as a private in the United States Marine Corps.

*   *   *

Part V

27

Life as a Recruit in the United States Marine Corps

I had my ticket for the train that was to leave in about an hour from Baltimore for Parris Island, South Carolina—a place I had never heard of, although it was in my home state. There was a four-hour delay in Washington, and I ran into a small group of boys who had enlisted in D.C. They were going on the same train to the same destination. One man had all the orders for his group and he thought I should turn my orders over to him, but I saw no reason to do this and kept my orders until we got to Parris Island. It was the day before Franklin D. Roosevelt's second inauguration. The stands had been built in front of the Capitol building, and we climbed around on them like kids. About six o'clock we went to the railroad station and boarded the train. While I was on the train I decided to wear my boots and riding britches, which was not a smart thing to do, as it made me look different from the other recruits and the military didn't like that.

The Recruits Have Landed at P.I.

The train stopped at Port Royal, which is just across the bay from Parris Island. We rode a boat to the landing at P.I. There was a road and bridge, but I never saw them until

Platoon 2, Marine Barracks, Parris Island, South Carolina

years later. We were allowed to eat, and after that they started giving us the works. They clipped off all our hair and issued us new outfits, pajamas, and utility clothing, which didn't fit very well. As I was turning in my civilian clothing a corporal asked me what I was going to do with my boots. I didn't think it would make any difference if I didn't give them to him, but it turned out later that he was an instructor for our platoon. He remembered me, and every time he came near he would hit me with his little swagger stick. It didn't leave any marks but was very painful, especially if he hit a finger when I was holding it on the rifle. There wasn't anything I could do about it. (*He was caught by the Japanese at the beginning of World War II. I saw him after the war, but I didn't speak to him. He was a warrant officer and I was a captain. He had survived almost four years as a Japanese prisoner.*)

Most of our instructors were dedicated people who worked long, hard hours. Promotions were slow and they used to say you were doing well if you got a promotion when you reenlisted. You were expected to make sergeant after eight years, but some would not get above a corporal in twenty years. *At one time on the West Coast there was a group who hung out together. To belong you had to have ten years or more as a corporal. Some of them had offenses of some kind, and some didn't care if they were promoted or not. They drank a lot and never married, maybe partially because a corporal was not entitled to family allowances. Sometimes they would move in with a woman, but most of them preferred to serve overseas.*

After I had been assigned to a platoon and had been training for a couple of weeks I was told that I would have to see the battalion commander. I was marched across the parade field and up to the battalion headquarters. The sergeant major had my service record on his desk, and he marched me into the office of the battalion commander. I had no idea what was going on, but they told me that my pay would be stopped and that I would probably be kicked out of the Corps. He wanted to know what I had to say about fraudulently enlisting. *The recruiting sergeant had asked me when I enlisted if I had ever been convicted of any crime. I had not been convicted of any crime. When I was hoboing around the country I had been picked up but released after being checked out.* The colonel wanted to know if I wanted to remain in the service or wanted a discharge. I would have preferred to leave but instead said I would like to remain in the service, which apparently was the right thing to say, because they let me continue on with the platoon. They finally told me weeks later that I could remain in the Corps, and they started paying me again.

We had to attend Sunday services; nobody was excused. It is probably different now, but we were marched in and seated and had to remain until dismissed. The chaplain didn't seem to have a high regard for recruits. He would say: "Remember, spirits bright, minds alert, and bodies clean." I suppose he thought enlisted men were not accustomed to bathing.

28

Rifle Range—Fleas—Drill Instructor

Toward the later part of our training we marched out to the rifle range and trained for firing the range for record. They had eased up a bit on the pressure, and the duties were a little lighter. At times we would be in what was called the Butts. You pulled the targets up, and they would fire from different ranges. There was a corporal in charge. He must have weighed over three hundred pounds. I never saw him in a regular uniform. He was always dressed in utility clothing. It was said that he had to combine two belts together to reach around his waist. He had a two-wheeled cart that he would sprawl out on, but when he saw an officer coming he would get out of the cart and start harassing the troops operating the targets. He carried a stick with him and would threaten to use it on anyone not doing the job. I don't believe he ever struck anyone with it. *This corporal had been stationed in Cuba before he came to Parris Island. His job had been taking care of the farm and raising hogs. He met and married a local woman there. She was attractive, and she might have married him to get to the States. I saw her in Quantico, Virginia, a couple of years later. I don't know how he managed to reenlist. If you were a sergeant you were supposed to be eligible for reenlistment, and he probably couldn't have passed a physical examination. It seemed that the corps would tolerate a few characters. Almost every company in the Fourth Regiment in China had at least one person who had to be hidden during inspections. When*

I retired, most of the characters had been pushed out. If you didn't get promoted when you had been in grade a certain length of time, you could not reenlist.

One time we were marched to an area where there were lots of sand fleas. We were called to attention, and the fleas started to work. They were all over us, and we were not allowed to move or to swat them. I guess that was part of a tradition, and eventually it was used in a book that was made into a movie. *In stories or movies about the Marine Corps the sergeants would get right up in the faces of the recruits when they were inspecting the troops. I have discussed this with marines who were in the service before the war, and they tell me they never saw anything like that.*

We fired the range and returned to the barracks. We were issued a complete outfit of uniforms, including dress blues. This uniform was not comfortable, and most of the troops usually went on liberty in civilian clothes. When we had our platoon picture made we were wearing campaign hats and our winter service green uniforms.

29

A Delay in Leaving the Island

We were about ready to leave the island but had to have a physical inspection. It didn't amount to much. I was talking to the naval doctor who was doing the physical, and he asked me if I had any problems. I said I did not. I was looking at one of the men in the platoon who had large jaws and was a bit plump around the neck, and for no reason at all, I told the doctor that Private Flowers had the mumps. The examining doctor perked up at this new bit of information. He decided to put us in quarantine, which meant we would be held back for about three weeks. There were a lot of unhappy marines, and if they had known I was the reason for this snafu I would have been in big trouble. Our training was completed, but they put us to work cleaning up an area on the waterfront. It was like a jungle, but we cleared it with axes and saws. *Later, they discovered this was where the French settlers, under the leadership of a man named Ribault, had tried to establish a settlement there. It had failed and they had to build a boat to try to get home. Some of the men died. A few made it back to France. Now there are markers where the settlement was located.*

One day two of us missed the working party and went to a movie. We were picked up by the police and had to go up for office hours before the battalion commander. Since we were about ready to leave they just entered a statement in our service record book. I probably had several offenses later on, but this was the only one on record. We finally got word to pack up and get ready to leave the island. We had no parade or anything else. *Present-day recruit graduations are fine ceremonies. I have been back a few times and found them very impressive. The band plays and the troops parade. Some make PFC at graduation. It took me over three years for my first promotion.*

30

Leaving Parris Island at Last

When we got word to get ready to move out there was a collection for the drill instructor, but I didn't contribute. We departed the same way we came in. We crossed over by boat to Port Royal to catch the train. There was a wait before we could go on board. An old marine with an accent approached us and said he could get some whiskey for us and if we would give him the money he would put it on board the train. *He had been a sergeant but had gotten mixed up in some kind of bootlegging at Quantico and had been reduced to private. I heard him say that if he could have played a bugle they would have made him a "music." At that time "music" was supposed to be the lowest rank.* He stood by the tracks as we departed. He was waving and smiling. He had collected several dollars, but he had not put any whiskey on board the train.

Some of the men from our platoon had orders for overseas, and a few had orders for duty on ships. I had enlisted because I wanted to see foreign stations, but I would be stuck in Quantico, Virginia, for the next two years.

*   *   *

Part VI

31

Marine Barracks, Quantico, Virginia—1937

A group of us from Parris Island arrived in Quantico in the spring of 1937. We were sent to various units. I was in C Company, First Battalion, Fifth Marine Regiment. There were only three regiments in the Marine Corps at that time: the Fifth, the Sixth Regiment in San Diego, California, and the Fourth Regiment in China. All together there were about seventeen thousand marines—less than the New York police force. About half of the Corps was aboard battleships or cruisers or in navy yards. There were two major generals in Quantico at that time. One was called Haircut Charley. He was strict about how long or short your hair should be. The other general was known as Guard Mount Willy. He wanted a sharp performance every time, including formal guard mount. It was the old drill, several movements and with the regimental band. If he didn't like it, you would hear about it at foot locker inspection. He was concerned mostly about clean mirrors.

The colonel of the regiment was called Smiling Sam. He had never been known to smile. If you were bald you would be called Curly. Lots of the old-timers had nicknames. A fat person might be known as Tiny. Indians were Chief or Papoose. We spent the summer out in the field holding operations and on lots of drills. One hot day in July we were in the field reenacting some battle. We were crawling around on the ground advancing against the imaginary enemy when the battalion EXO called out, "Stop picking berries! You are under fire!" The troops thought that was very funny, and for days they would call out, "Stop picking berries!"

In the fall we lived in tents out near Manassas, Virginia, near one of the battlegrounds of the Civil War. We were equipped with World War I gear. There wouldn't be anything new until World War II began four years later. Our company commander had not had a promotion in fourteen years and wanted to impress the battalion CO. He was always volunteering our company to do the dirty work when we broke camp, and we usually did it. Some would always call out, "Let C Company do it!" He was a pleasant fellow, but I don't believe he had a command in combat during the war. It was amazing that most World War II generals were highly qualified. Someone apparently knew who should and should not have a high command. Of course there were exceptions, but most of them were highly qualified.

32

Training in Puerto Rico, 1938

In January the regiment moved aboard ship for training in Puerto Rico. Our company was aboard the battleship *New York*. We left Norfolk when temperatures were below freezing, and every day it got warmer. We passed by Cape Hatteras when waves were coming up over the bow. It was peacetime and we had to sleep anywhere we could find. At that time there was no landing craft except the ones that belonged to the ship. We were probably in the way of the crew. Someone was always hollering, "You can't sit here, marines!"

We arrived in Puerto Rico on the seventh day and prepared for a landing on a small island called Culebra. In Spanish this means "snake." We climbed down the side of the ship on nets that had been placed there and into the boats. We landed as we would have under combat conditions. (*Four years later the First Marine Division landed on Guadalcanal, but by then there were several types of landing crafts, one of which was the amphibian tractor. This vehicle was able to operate on land and sea.*) The first operation was cut short so that camp could be set up. It was the first time I had slept in a tent, but it wouldn't be the last. It was something to leave Norfolk in the middle of winter and land on a tropical island with palm trees and white sandy beaches.

As soon as we got camp set up we started training. I was the smallest man in the eight-man squad, so they made me the bar man. BAR is an abbreviation for Browning Automatic

Rifle. It weighs about fifteen pounds, about double the 1903 rifle, but I could manage.

Sometimes we attacked the island, and at other times we defended. They would put down a smokescreen, and we would come ashore. We put up huge targets for the navy. They would fire all the ship's guns, including the sixteen-inch guns. It was very impressive. We could fire our small arms at various targets. We even fired at targets that were towed by airplanes. We operated in some rough terrain, but I think most of us enjoyed it. It wasn't all work and no play.

We got liberty in St. Thomas, San Juan, and Martinique. The lower enlisted grades had to be back aboard the ship at midnight. They called it Cinderella Liberty Senior. NCOs and officers were allowed to stay out all night. We had tours on Martinique. The volcano was still smoking at that time. We saw the town of St. Pierre. *It had been destroyed several years earlier by the volcano called Pelé. Only one man had survived, and he was a prisoner in an underground prison.* The language in Martinique was French. A franc was about the same value as a quarter. A franc would buy a bottle of champagne.

One morning a craft from the town came up to our ship. They came aboard and a woman was with them. She complained that she had been cheated by a marine who had given her some kind of coupon and convinced her that it was American money. She said the man had two stripes and a mustache. All corporals with mustaches were mustered on deck, but she couldn't identify the man and I believe the complaint was dropped.

The French liner *Normandy* was in port, and she was a beautiful ship. As she was pulling out, a group in a small boat chased her. Some of the passengers were about to be left behind. They couldn't catch up and had to return to port.

We went back to camp in Culebra and resumed maneuvers in the hills. One day two of us went hiking in the hills. We came to a small clearing where there was a house of a kind. It had dirt floors and straw walls and roof. There were goats and a few chickens and a banana plant. I don't know how those people survived, but they seemed to be making out. The man was glad to have visitors, but he couldn't speak English. I knew a few words in Spanish, and I would point to an object and he would say what it was in Spanish. He had a windup Victrola but only one record. It was in English. The record was about Lindbergh. I believe it was called "Lindbergh, the Lone Eagle of the USA." He would play this record over and over and roar with laughter.

There was a nice beach where we went swimming until one man was bitten by a barracuda. They decided to close the beach to the enlisted and let the officers take chances if they wanted to swim anyway. Guards were posted to enforce the order. One of the privates asked the sergeant of the guard how he distinguished an officer from an enlisted man. The question didn't faze the sergeant. He said, "You can tell by the intelligent expressions on the officers' faces." Sergeants had answers for every occasion.

33

Return to Marine Barracks, Quantico

About the end of March we returned to Marine Barracks, Quantico. We returned on the *New York* to Norfolk and took the train back to the base. I had traveled in all the states and had crossed the country several times, but I had enlisted for travel and adventure and wanted to go to China. My request was denied because I had not been in the company two years. I was able to get transferred to the First Tank Company, but these tanks were not anything like the ones that came later. They had very light armor and one .50-caliber machine gun and two .30-caliber. However, the duty was different. When we went in the field we rode, and in the barracks we had fewer drills and inspections.

34

Operations on Vieques—1939

The following winter operations were held on a different island. We traveled on an old cargo ship named the *Antereas*. We carried the tanks along, but the real purpose was to see how we held up in field operations. The name of the island was Vieques. The only town was named Isabel Segunda. The island had more population than Culebra. I don't remember seeing any restaurants, but there were two or three taverns. Rum was about the only thing served. One brand was called Palo Viejo or, in English, Old Tree. It was cheap and it reminded me of the corn whiskey made in our southern mountains. I had a few drinks and didn't feel that I had overdone it. However, when I stepped out of the cool, dark tavern into the bright, hot sunshine it was a different story. A second lieutenant on patrol put me in the truck and carried me back to camp. The lieutenant said that he benefited by seeing me in this condition and thus was careful not to drink too much rum. (*In later years I ran into him and he reminded me of that occasion. The last time I saw him was in Tsingtao, China, after the war, and he was a bird colonel.*)

Some days later I was back in town and didn't return on time. I was going to be over leave, so I thought I could get in without being seen. I circled the camp and came into what the marines called the head, the idea being I would pretend I hadn't been away. I made it to my tent and thought I had gotten away with it, but the sergeant of the guard was sitting on my bunk. We knew each other, but that didn't make any difference. The next day I was up for Office Hours and expected to get the works. Fortunately, a warrant officer in my company knew the colonel and had talked with him, so I ended up by getting a warning.

35

Return to Quantico, Extend Enlistment, and Drive across Country with Sergeant Neal—Destination Mare Island, California

We got back to Quantico, but I wasn't satisfied about not getting duty overseas. Again I put in a letter asking for China duty. They wrote back and said I was not eligible because I had less than two years to complete my enlistment and that I would have to extend for an additional year if I wanted to go. I had not planned to stay in the service beyond my original four years, but I thought about it a day or two and then went down to the sergeant's office and extended.

Another man in the company, Sergeant Neal, got his orders for China at the same time. He had a car and was driving across country. Back then you could get a furlough transfer but no travel allowance. It was better than riding on a slow transport through the Panama Canal. When leaving a station you had to check out. This was easy if they found out you didn't owe anything. When I got to the last stop an officer gave me clearance and then said, "You are as good as on Bubbling Well Road." *That was the first time I had heard that name, but I was to know it well in the months ahead.*

Sergeant Neal and I left Quantico and drove straight through to Montana, where his family lived. We stopped only for food and gas. When Sergeant Neal left home to join the

Marine Corps his family had been living in Iowa. I don't think he had seen his folks since he enlisted twelve years before. He had been overseas much of that time and had been a first lieutenant in the Nicaraguan Guard. He had ribbons and chevrons and he looked pretty good when he went out on Sundays. I had no medals, stripes, or anything, but the local people were very friendly. I don't know if they had ever seen a marine in that part of the country. We stayed most of the thirty days on the farm. They had some land that was irrigated and some that was not. They planted wheat on the uplands hoping this area would get enough snow to provide moisture. I think they missed about half the time. Sergeant Neal got on the tractor and started plowing. I fished for trout and had a job shooting prairie dogs. They would dig holes in the pasture, and sometimes a cow or horse would step in it and break a leg. I got several. When you approached them they would disappear down the hole, but if you waited they would come back up. All it took was a little patience.

36

Travel on to California and Mare Island Navy Yard

We stayed on the farm until about three days before time to check in at Mare Island Navy Yard. We had a short drive the first day. Upon entering Stone Park, we stopped at the gate and the park ranger spotted our rifles. (At that time marines were issued a rifle at boot camp and kept it until they were discharged.) The ranger was alarmed. He probably thought we intended to shoot some of the animals. He said he would put seals on the triggers so they couldn't be fired. After finding out we were marines he said that wouldn't be necessary, but Sergeant Neal insisted the seals be put on. It was early May, but snow was on the ground and some was still falling. We spent the first night in the lodge and saw the Old Faithful geyser do its thing, and right on schedule.

The next day we drove to Reno. It was a small town, but at that time they had Harrah's Gambling Casino and a place called the Bull Pen. There were lots of women in Reno getting divorces. At that time it was the "divorce capital" of the country. I think they had to wait six weeks. Most of the states were not that liberal, and in some places it was almost impossible to obtain a divorce. The next day we drove the rest of the way. At the California line they were stopping and searching all cars. They were trying to discourage people without money from entering the state. The excuse for stopping people was to keep out the Mediterranean fruit fly. I gave him a hard time and advised him not to hold up marines travel-ing under orders. He didn't like it, but he let us go through without waiting in line.

37

Duty at Mare Island—Waiting for the *Chaumont*

We proceeded to Vallejo and rode the ferry to Mare Island. We checked in and were assigned Quarters. We were supposed to board the *Henderson*. She was an old troop transport from World War I. We were on time, but the marine detachment commanding officer was short of personnel, so he made us stay and wait for the next transport, the *Chaumont*. We had to wait about two months. We did guard duty, but we could get liberty in San Francisco. The World's Fair of 1939 was being held on Treasure Island, and liberty was always good in San Francisco. A few days after we checked in I was standing guard at the brig. I started talking to a marine I had known in Quantico who was currently a prisoner. Neal was sergeant of the guard, and he heard me talking to the prisoner. Neal said very quietly that if I wanted to talk to a prisoner he would put me in a cell with him. Sergeant Neal and I were friends, but there are no friends when you are on duty. I had no doubt that if I were caught I would be locked up. It was a good lesson. The next day we were off and Neal asked me if I wanted to go to the World's Fair and I was relieved to know he was not going to stay upset about the incident.

Liberty in San Francisco

We stopped in San Francisco the first night after leaving Mare Island, and they let us have liberty. I was about broke, but I went ashore anyway. As I was walking down the street I was approached by two women. I could tell that they were not prostitutes. It seemed they wanted to see some nightlife and didn't want to go without an escort. I told them I appreciated the offer, but I couldn't afford it and, being a southern gentleman, would have to refuse. They were persistent, but they were nice people from the Midwest—a woman and her daughter-in-law. They wanted to see the gay bars. We went to Mona's and Pinocchios. If I remember correctly, Mona's had lesbians. They danced with each other and wore strange clothing. Mona's served drinks and had entertainers. Then we went to Pinocchio's, where the men were all paired off and dancing. I guess the midwestern ladies had a lot to talk about when they got back to town. The evening ended about midnight, and they got a cab and went with me to the ship. We said good-bye and they thanked me. These two nice ladies were the last American women I would talk to for two years.

38

Sailing on the *Chaumont*—Destination China

We sailed the following morning. The water was rough and a lot of the passengers got sick. There were a number of sailors who were going to sea for the first time. Most of them got really sick. Fewer of the marines who were on their first voyage got sick. I suppose the sailors had been told about how bad it was going to be and that made the situation worse. I had the brig watch the first night and didn't get sick, but I had been in the Atlantic and had passed through Cape Hatteras in the winter when the waves were really rough. The waters were much calmer after we got farther away from the coast. I got assigned duty as the captain's orderly. Three of us stood the watches, which meant that we would be wherever the captain was, so for eight hours a day we would be up where the air was better. The watch was around-the-clock. At night we stood by the captain's quarters. Orderlies were the only ones, except the ship's executive, who could enter the captain's room. All others had to be announced. The captain made it clear that if he was needed he wanted to be awakened, even if he had to be shaken. About midway to Hawaii the captain held services for the ashes of a retired naval officer. The ship was stopped while this was going on. This could cause the ship to drift and get off course. The captain had told me that immediately after the last rites I was to get to the bridge and inform the officer of the watch to proceed. I was a little slow, and the captain was quite irked with me. It was the only time I saw him lose his temper.

Stops at Oahu, Midway Island, Guam, and Manila Bay

The seventh day, we approached Oahu. We came in sight of Diamond Head. A few hours later we pulled to the pier and tied up. There were hula dancers on the dock dancing and singing and passing out leis. The main performer called herself Hilo Hattie. One song was about a princess who liked to give it away. The reason we got all this attention was because there was not much going on in 1939. We were allowed to go ashore, but it was like the old saying: "You have liberty, but there are no boats." We did go ashore, but most of us didn't have enough money to do any celebrating. We could walk around the beach, but people knew that privates made only twenty-one dollars a month and couldn't do much buying. I ended up at the YMCA and wrote a couple of letters. I think everyone was ready to move on. We still had a long way to go. We stopped at Midway Island and anchored outside but didn't go ashore. We dropped off a couple of civilians who were to be there for six months. One marine decided he had gone far enough, so he tried to jump ship. They grabbed him and locked him in the ship's brig. I never saw him again, but he was probably put off at the next stop, which was Guam.

At that time Guam was not considered a good duty post. We knew that a few of us would be put off there. There was one volunteer who had been sick all the way. He said he was going to stay on Guam until he could save enough money to buy a ticket on the China Clipper. These planes could cross the Pacific in about four days. One of the stops was at

106

Guam. This marine said he wanted to fly over the *Chaumont* and drop a bag of chicken poop on the ship. I never saw him again.

We went ashore at Agana, then a small town on the island. There were only a few hundred people living there at that time. The navy was in charge, and a navy captain was the governor. The idea was to run the place like a state ship. One of the former governors had issued an order forbidding anyone from whistling. The people didn't seem to be oppressed. They were a gentle people. (*Five years later I would return with the Third Marine Division to retake the island.*) We stayed in Agana a couple of days. I went ashore the second night and celebrated by drinking some of the local brand of coconut juice. I returned to the ship carrying a watermelon and dropped it when I came on deck. It splattered and this displeased the officer of the day and he wrote up a report. The only consequence was that I lost my job as captain's orderly. I was assigned duty in the chief's mess. The chiefs knew how to live. They had the best food on the ship. They also tipped the mess men. I managed to save enough to get into the illegal gambling that went on. I won about forty dollars, and that was about two month's pay. The money came in handy when I had to buy China khaki. (*The regular-issue khaki clothing wasn't worn in the Fourth Regiment. I don't know if we could have been forced to wear the trousers that hadn't been issued, but it was better to go along with the policy. Besides, they fit better and looked good.*)

We arrived in Manila Bay about a week later and were allowed to go ashore. Most of the city was dirty and overcrowded, but we were off the ship. We rode in horse-drawn vehicles, went to cockfights, and ended up in a nightclub. I think the name was Dreamland—anyway, the biggest one around. *There was an old lady there who had a story to tell. She claimed that she had had sexual relations with Admiral Dewey and that he was her first. It could have happened, she would have been about the right age, but it was probably something she made up.*

We left the Philippines and I was sure glad not to be assigned duty there. The Fourth Regiment was big on athletics, and they wanted ball players. I put my name on the list, but my only experience was in the little one-room school I attended and I think that saved me.

I don't know why I was lucky enough to get my job back as captain's orderly, but I was happy about that, too. It was good to be up where the air was better. We continued on our way to China.

Some of the officers and their wives would sleep outside their cabins. One night when it was a little rough a sentry walked by and stumbled against the bunk of one of the women. She claimed that she thought he was trying to rape her. They asked if she was sure about what happened, and she finally agreed that it could have been accidental. If she had stuck to her story the marine would have been sent to naval prison. As we approached Formosa (now the name is Taiwan) the captain got nervous because the Japanese held the island and relations were not good even in 1939. A small Japanese craft got between us and the island and stayed there until we had cleared the island. I think the captain was glad when we got past the place.

*   *   *

Part VII

39

Arrival in Shanghai, China

A few days later we ran into the Yellow Sea. We knew then that we were approaching China. The following day we pulled into port at Shanghai. It was a sight to see. There were sampans in the river. Laborers were on the dock. The streets were filled with coolies pulling rickshas. A group from regimental headquarters was waiting. They were distributing our people out to one of the two battalions. I don't know why he did it, but the first battalion sergeant major picked me for First Battalion Headquarters. It may have been because I had pressed khaki. The captain's orderlies could use the ship's laundry. The others had to do their laundry in salt water, and their clothes didn't look very good. The marines meeting us really looked sharp. Their khaki was tailored, starched, and pressed. They wore sun helmets and most carried swagger sticks.

They loaded us on the trucks and delivered us to our billets. They let us have the rest of the day to get settled in. As soon as we got inside, a room boy took charge. I put down my sea bag, pack, and rifle and took a bath in fresh water. (For over a month the baths had been in salt water, and I never really felt clean.) In the meantime the room boy had made up the bunk with clean linen and had gathered up all my dirty clothes for the laundry. The only thing we were required to do was clean our rifles. I knew I had come to the right place. After an afternoon siesta we put on the clean clothes and went to the mess hall. After we ate we went to the enlisted club. We were issued a club book that we could use for food and drink. It turned out that on the first night I was supposed to treat marines from my company until the book was closed. It amounted to a half-month's pay.

Around eleven o'clock almost everyone left the club and went to nightclubs or cafés. Some had girlfriends. Most of the places stayed open all night. They were so hard up that they gave credit to just about anyone. They let us sign a chit, so most jokers would sign the colonel's name. They had clubs that were Russian, French, and other nationalities. There were cafés and bars of other countries. Liberty was up at six o'clock in the morning, but we needed to get in, change clothes, and fall out for exercises.

40

Report for Duty

The next day I reported to the sergeant major to work in the message center. My job was to pick up official mail from regimental headquarters, bring it back to the battalion, and if necessary take it to the companies. If we were in the field I would be the battalion CO's runner. It was an easy job. The sergeant major's name was Frederick. He was German. *One day a lieutenant asked Frederick if he had served in the German army. He replied that it was none of his business. Another time the company first sergeant, who had been drinking during working hours, came into the office and leaned on his desk. The sergeant major asked, "Why are you leaning on my desk? Didn't you eat breakfast? Now go away and don't come back unless I send for you."* Most everyone steered clear of him. The colonel was called Donald Duck by the troops. I don't know why. I thought he was an officer and a gentleman. The executive officer was called Whiskey Bill.

Over in the second battalion the CO was called the Mad Monarch. *He had ordered that people should not use more than twelve squares of toilet paper. He always looked at the back of shoes at inspections. He said that anyone who didn't shine the back of his shoes probably didn't wipe his ass. He looked like a kind and gentle old man. A man going up for office hours would think that he was going to hear a good story and get off with a warning, but the Mad Monarch always lowered the boom. He would smile and say, "Good morning, son," and then order sum-mary court-martial. This could mean almost anything—a reduc-tion in rank, thirty days in the brig, and if he felt like it he could add bread and water. He said he had to do it and that if he didn't God would punish him. (I was glad that I never served in his outfit. In World War II he was relieved as a CO of an engineer battalion.)* After I had been in the regiment for a few weeks I brought a little food from the mess hall and gave it to a beggar outside the gate. A sergeant saw me do this and called me over to his side of the street. He said, "I know you mean well, but there are a million people starving in Shanghai. They have fled the Japanese. If you start doing this you will have hundreds of beggars around." He was right. It was a bad situation.

One of the marines wrote to a magazine called *Lonely Hearts.* He wrote: "I'm a lonely marine in war-torn China." We were living in the fourth-largest city in the world. There was no danger in the city. The fighting was all outside the international city limits. Somebody read the article and whenever he showed up someone would say, "I'm a lonely marine in war-torn China." It probably embarrassed him, but he got letters from the United States and when he got back he had some names and addresses.

International Forces, Shanghai, China, 1939

Soochow Creek, Shanghai, China, 1939

American Marine and Japanese Sentry, Shanghai, China, 1939

Great Wall of China (Jack Wright on left), 1939

Great Wall of China (Jack Wright), 1939

41

Deplorable Conditions

One day when I was making my rounds I saw a coolie carrying a bucket of hot rice on what we called a Ya Hog pole. The reason we called it that was what they said when going through the woods. It meant "let me through." There was a bucket on each end of the pole. He let a bucket fall on the street. A begger started grabbing the rice and cramming it in his mouth. The coolie started beating him with the pole, but he wouldn't stop. Blood was running down his arm and into the rice, but he kept on eating. When we walked a couple of blocks to the mess hall we would walk around the dead and dying. After a while we got used to all this. It was a place of contrast. We could see a fat Chinaman pass by in a limousine with chauffeur and bodyguards. Their homes had walls with broken glass on top. Some had Sikh watchmen. These men had beards and turbans. They were mostly over six feet tall, and the poor Chinese were afraid of them. The only organization I saw doing anything was the Salvation Army, and they couldn't do a whole lot. I saw women having babies on the sidewalks. There were too many people.

42

I Get in Trouble

I was at the club one Saturday night when a marine flyman came in. He was stationed on the USS *Augusta*. We started making the rounds and ended up in a section of town called Blood Alley. It was in-bounds for the ship's marines, but it was out-of-bounds for marines of the Fourth Regiment. We hadn't been there ten minutes before the shore patrol grabbed me. The marine from the ship tried to talk them out of taking me in. I knew it wouldn't work, and I didn't want to add to my offense. If you caused trouble, they would beat you when they locked you up. The brig was called Mawbell Mansion, and it was tough. I stayed locked up until Monday morning. Then I was brought up before the battalion CO. I was expecting a court-martial, which could be pretty bad, but I think the colonel liked me. I had served in his outfit before, and after talking it over with the sergeant major the colonel decided since this was my first offense they would transfer me to a company. He seemed concerned about me and didn't put anything in my service record, but he said, "I don't want to see you again." This was a letdown, going from battalion headquarters to a line company. I'm not one of these people who think everything happens for the best, but I learned a lot and was better off in a lot of things I needed to know.

I was made a squad leader. I didn't want the job, because it wouldn't mean a promotion, and it meant that I would be harassed by a second lieutenant who was a USNA graduate. He would pretend to find something wrong with one of my men and ask me if I had checked the men before they fell out for formation. There was no right answer. If I had checked them it was: "Why didn't you correct the problem?" and if I had not checked them it was: "Why didn't you check them?" This was something he had learned at the academy. My main concern was having fun, and liberty call was one o'clock. This gave us lots of time to take in the sights.

One day I was standing watch at the naval hospital. No one was allowed out without a pass. A patient came and asked if he could go out to a house next door. He had a girlfriend there. He was in uniform, but he didn't have his liberty card. I knew better, but I let him out anyway. A few minutes later he was brought back by the MPs, and I had to see the battalion CO. The marine had gone next door to a whorehouse that was out-of-bounds. He was really in trouble, and it looked like I was also. The battalion CO questioned him first. He immediately tried to make me responsible for saying that I had let him out the gate. I didn't like his attitude, and when I was asked if that was true I lied and said I hadn't seen him before and if he had gotten out while I was on duty he must have climbed over the fence. I don't know if they believed my story, but they didn't charge me with anything. I never regretted lying about it. It could have been very serious for me. I don't think I ever did anything like that again.

43

Japanese Soldiers and Soochow Creek

One day while on guard on Soochow Creek, which was the border with the Japanese, I saw some Japanese soldiers beating up some refugees. They were removing the refugees from under the bridge where they were camped. They didn't like for us to observe them doing this, and they motioned for us to get back. We ignored this because we were in the international part of the city. Finally an officer got a few men together, and drawing his sword he started running toward us. If he expected to scare us away, he was wrong. I'm not fearless and later during the war I was often frightened. I had a loaded rifle, but the other marine with me had not loaded. I told him to go into the guard shack and load. He did, but while loading he had an accidental discharge. This could have started something, but it didn't. The Japanese stopped and returned to their side of the creek, but I had to report the accidental discharge to the officer of the day and he came out on a motorcycle. Officers were driven in on a motorcycle with a side car. He gave a little talk saying that any incident could cause international repercussions. He liked to use big words. After I got off guard I was told to report to regimental headquarters. I had to tell my story to the regimental commander. He made no comment and I didn't hear any more about it.

Standing watch on Soochow Creek was a real ordeal, because this was where the "honey carts" put their loads of human fertilizer on barges to take to the countryside to be used in the fields. They usually arrived about 4:00 A.M. and didn't finish until 6:00 A.M. or later. I don't think they had any regular fertilizer.

44

Go to Ch'in-huang-tao—1940

In May we got ready to go to the rifle range in Ch'in-huang-tao. A Company was the only one to go. It was good duty. We fired the rifle range and did light work, stood some watches, and could spend lots of time on the beach. Ch'in-huang-tao is where the Great Wall ends. Manchuria is on the north of the wall. We were not supposed to go out of the camp area because the Japanese were in control of all the surrounding area. We went out often, and no one bothered us. We saw Japanese soldiers using horse-drawn artillery and thought that they weren't much of a threat to the United States. (*They were probably underrated then and were overrated for a while after Pearl Harbor.*) One day we walked down the railroad and came to a bridge that was guarded by a Japanese sentry. He pointed a rifle at us and motioned us back, but he let us get close enough to grab his rifle and take it away from him. He started smiling then and we took a picture of us together. We also visited the girls who had been brought out to service the troops. They were clean, bright, and pretty, and I don't think they felt any shame or embarrassment about what they were doing. It was my belief that prostitution was considered an honorable profession in the Orient.

45

Back at Camp

When we arrived in camp the first thing I noticed was our room boy. Loo had beaten us there and had our tent ready. The cots were made up. I don't know how he had managed it. I guess he had ridden the train. He was much brighter than the other boys and could speak pretty good English. One time when we were about to go into town he said to me, "Maybe more better you don't go. You only got one stripe. If you lose that you got nothing." We had a man who couldn't manage his liquor. He would go out in the afternoon, and before it even got dark he would be brought back to the barracks. His name was Belcher. When we got ready to go on liberty the room boy would say, "Now don't make a Belcher out of yourself." He worried about us like a father, but he wasn't much older than we were.

It was 1940 and there was war in Europe, but it seemed far away and we didn't worry about it. It would be a very long time before there was another summer like this. *The next summer in Shanghai things would tighten up. We would have to wear our uniforms on liberty, and liberty was up at midnight. Also, we had alerts and standbys. At times I would be out on the streets with my squad. I was armed with a loaded Thompson submachine gun. The men had rifles with fixed bayonets. We had orders to keep the streets open. It was probably instigated by the Japanese. Everything had changed.*

46

Liberty in Peking

Meanwhile we were having a good summer up north, and before returning to Shanghai we would have eight days' liberty in Peking. We rode there by train and stayed in the Legations Barracks. The Peking marines were famous. They were known as the "Horse Marines," because, naturally, they patrolled on horses. *I knew some of them, and I met one I had gone through boot camp with and had known in Quantico. I asked him why he had been transferred. He said that he had been taking care of the officers' horses and one day a colonel brought his horse back to the stables and instructed my friend about taking care of his mount. He was to walk him and let him cool off. Then he was to groom and put some feed out. My friend said, "Yes, sir," and "Aye-aye sir." The colonel pretended to leave, but he was just around the corner. My friend thought he had gone, so he took the saddle and bridle off and slapped the horse on the rear with the reins. The colonel had him cold. It is not clear as to what happened, but he had to serve five days on bread and water. After that he wanted to get as far away as he could from Quantico.* He and I went out to a café that was a hangout for Japanese officers. He said, "I will buy one of them a drink of sake and he will offer to buy us a drink, and I will ask for scotch." The sake was cheap. The scotch cost at least double. The officers didn't hang around much after that.

The toilets were unisex, men and women at the same time, and no one seemed concerned. It was strange to have countries that were fighting each other having troops going on liberty together. Later Colonel Turnage, who was CO, Marine Barracks, set alternate days for the British and Italians to have liberty. We had to check in at eight in the mornings, and after that we were free until the next day. It was miserably hot and there was no air-conditioning. One night we went to the French monastery and bought several bottles of champagne. They probably cost about twenty-five cents each. We had ricksha boys with us, and they found some buckets and ice. We sneaked into the Forbidden City and stayed until morning. It was much cooler than the barracks. The ricksha boys in Peking were different from the ones in Shanghai. Some of them were college students and could speak English. It seemed odd to have a ricksha boy explain Chinese history. We visited the summer palace and other places in the area. The story about the Marble Boat was that the empress got money to build a navy but spent it all on the boat. Maybe she did the right thing, because the boat is still there. She collected a lot of clocks and an ancient automobile. She had covered walkways around the palace. She could go outside and not be in the sun or rain.

47

Return to Ch'in-huang-tao

We returned by train to Ch'in-huang-tao and the rifle range a couple of days later. It was a lot cooler along the beach, and we swam almost every day. It was almost like a vacation, and we had a chance to see the Great Wall and ride donkeys along the top. We had pictures made by a Chinaman with an old-fashioned camera mounted on a tripod. The wall comes all the way to the sea. The Manchurian border is on the other side. *The Japanese had occupied it in the early 1930s and renamed it Manchuro.*

48

Return to Shanghai

We returned to Shanghai about the last of August. We rode back on the USS *Augusta*. When we came up the Whangpoo we passed the Japanese flag ship. On the topside they were doing the routine of dipping the flag and saluting below decks. Below decks U.S. marines and sailors in one ship and the Japanese sailors in another ship were shaking their fists at each other through the portholes.

A story circulated that at one time a Japanese ship got in the way of the *Augusta* and the U.S. admiral signaled them to move and told them if they didn't he would blow them out of the way. Whether or not it happened, it was a good story. The Japanese sentries would try to stop us when we crossed their lines to get to the rifle range. Some of the drivers wouldn't stop. A man named Ponvavage would never stop. He kept going and at the last minute the Japanese would jump out of the road. There was crossing for foot traffic and rickshas, and all Chinese had to stop and bow to the sentry. Anyone riding would have to stop and dismount. The Japanese wouldn't hesitate to beat the Chinese with a club or slap them.

I was in Honkew one night with another marine. We were not supposed to be there, as that was out-of-bounds. The man with me got in an argument with a shopkeeper and he called the Japanese police and they locked the man up. I thought I had finally gotten into real trouble. We were locked up with unwashed Orientals and no idea of how to get out. After we had been locked up for about an hour they wanted to know if we would pay a small fine. We would have given them all we had to get back to the other side. My friend was a tough coal miner from the mountains of West Virginia. (*Later when I was not with him he got in trouble with the MPs. I think they beat him and instead of locking him up they let him out at the barracks. This was a big mistake, because he got his rifle, loaded it, and went to the brig where the MPs were. I believe he would have killed them all. They saw him coming and tried to hide, but one of them stood by the door and grabbed the weapon. He was tried by general court-martial and got a long sentence. He was still in naval prison at Mare Island when I got back. I had written and he had to agree to let the warden read any letters he received. He refused and I doubt if he ever consented. I saw him across the fence one day and he called out, "Hey, you ear-banger!" That was because I had made PFC since I saw him. I don't know what happened to him. I hope they let him come back in the service after the war started. A lot of prisoners were reinstated.*)

49

Back in Shanghai

We were back in Shanghai and were standing guard and training. I learned a lot. We were allowed to act as NCOs and drill the platoon. There is something about hearing your own voice giving orders and having them obeyed that gives you confidence. We usually had two parades each week. One was by the battalion, and the other was the entire regiment. The band always played and we all complained, but I think most of us liked it. I suppose the idea was to show the flag and to let the people know that we were on the job. Actually, we were not prepared for a major war. We had no tanks or artillery, and the regiment had only a few hundred men. There were battalions during World War II that had more than that, but most of us believed we could whip the Japanese. One day we started out for the battalion parade. B Company was missing its company commander, I guess he had had a big night. After we had gone a short distance the captain came riding up in a ricksha. He caught up with his company, jumped out of the ricksha, drew his sword, and took his place at the head of B Company. I was recommended for promotion and took the test for corporal. The exams took three days and were directed by company commanders and some of the regiment staff officers. I passed the test, but there were not enough vacancies, so it was a year later that I got promoted. A corporal's job paid forty-two dollars per month.

132

50

Recalling Stories from the Shanghai Days

There were lots of stories told about U.S. civilians in Shanghai. One was about a man named E. T. Riley. He was supposed to have climbed over the wall of an Oklahoma state prison and ended up in Shanghai. He owned most of the slot machines. There were no Chinese coins that would work, so he made his own coins and had his name on them. I don't know if he got caught by the Japanese or not. As long as he was in Shanghai he was safe, but if he returned to the States they would put him back in prison. A radio announcer named Carroll was a well-known figure. He would give the Germans and Italians a hard time. He said the Italians had invented a new dance step; it was one step forward and two backward. This was when the Italians were being pushed back in North Africa. He told the German ladies to put away their victory dresses, that they wouldn't need them. He said that if the marines left he would be one jump ahead of them. He made it back all right. I heard him on the radio in 1942. He was broadcasting from a station in Ohio.

A couple used to visit the marine club. He was from somewhere in central Europe and had an accent. He was in civilian clothes one night, and a marine hearing him talk thought he was a refugee and asked him what he was doing in the club. He became very upset and said, "I'm a marine and have been for over twenty years." (A lot of the NCOs had served in World War I and after coming to the United

States enlisted and stayed in. The Marine Corps was the nearest thing to a Foreign Legion.) He and his girlfriend would take a table and order drinks. She would sit down and pull the table up to her. She wore a wig and one night she spilled some drinks and she took off the wig and mopped the table with it. He would take his false teeth out and put them in his drink. He didn't want anyone to steal his drink when he left the table.

We had a man who thought he could box. He worked out for weeks and he looked good, but on his first match he got hit by a Soviet fighter in the first round and knocked out. He had been bragging about what he could do and telling about how he couldn't fight outside the ring because his hands were lethal weapons. I think he gave up boxing after that one fight.

One weekend I had made plans for some partying. My girlfriend and I planned several things to do. It wasn't my turn for guard duty, but the company clerk had taken his friend's name off the list and put mine on it. It was too late to do anything about it, so that weekend I was standing watch on Soochow Creek down where the honey carts unloaded. To make it worse, a marine I knew had picked up my girlfriend and they came in a cab where I was standing watch. When I was relieved from duty I returned to the barracks and cleaned up, put on civilian clothes, and went looking for the company clerk. I found him sitting on the veranda at the clubhouse. I told him to get on his feet and started hitting him. He didn't want to fight, and I let him go. He could have reported it to the first sergeant and caused me some trouble, but he didn't because he knew he was wrong.

Everything was changing. There were lots of patrols and some incidents along Soochow Creek. We had to wear helmets on duty and they were old World War I types and very uncomfortable.

*   *   *

Part VIII

51

My Mother's Illness Calls Me Back to the United States—1941

I was due to rotate back to the United States but could have extended. I decided to return because my mother was in bad health and I hadn't been home for three years. I'm glad I didn't stay in China. If I had, I would have ended up as a prisoner of war. The next transport was the USS *Henderson*, another old World War I type but better than the *Chaumont*. It had more room on topside, and most of us stayed out as much as possible. We even slept on deck with just a blanket between us and the hard deck, but that was better than being below decks.

We boarded the *Henderson* and thought we would sail right away, but we had to wait a couple of days. They let us have shore leave, and I visited a girlfriend. *We had been going together for six months. She was a White Russian whose parents had escaped from the communists in Manchuria and lived in a place called Harbin. A lot of the refugees relocated there. The Russians had a hard time making a living because of the cheap Chinese labor and had to really scramble to exist. There were lots of them in China. I don't know how they managed after the Japanese took over.*

I returned to the ship. It was the last time I rode down Bubbling Well Road in a ricksha. *I returned to China five years later in 1945 but didn't get back to Shanghai.*

We sailed the following morning. We went down the Whangpoo to the Yangtse and out into the Yellow Sea. Some transports came back by Hong Kong. We returned by Manila. It wasn't considered a good liberty port. After China it seemed dull, and most of us didn't go far from the ship. The first day we let the Filipinos do some laundry for us. We had doubts about their honesty, but they brought the clothes back. We sent out some more to be laundered, and we never saw them again.

We left for Guam the next day. It took a few days to get there, and there wasn't much to do. There was a small marine detachment on the island. I went out to visit, but a typhoon had blown the upper floor off and some of the personnel were in tents. We only stayed three days and picked up a few of the marines to return to the United States. *Most Americans had never heard of these islands in the Central Pacific, but after the war started they were in the news.*

We continued on across the Pacific to Wake Island, but we anchored outside and no one went ashore. We picked up a couple of civilians. *I don't know why they were leaving, but they were lucky. The ones who stayed were Japanese POWs for a long time. They made the Japanese pay for the island by knocking out a few of their ships and we managed to hold them off for several days.* We crossed the International Date Line and gained the day we had lost going out.

52

Stop in Hawaii—1941

We came back to Hawaii, but it wasn't like it was in 1939. There were naval ships all over the place, and the ships were camouflaged with paint. Some of the ones I saw were the ones that would later be destroyed by the Japanese on December 7. We didn't tie up at the docks but came into Honolulu by the ship's boats. It would usually rain enough to wet you on the way in, but the sun would come out again right away. You would smell the flowers as you approached the shore. Our money didn't go far in Honolulu. We missed getting fifteen dollars for one as we had in China. (*In China we had felt more important. We were mostly bigger and better dressed and had some money to spend, and the white race still had a lot of prestige there. We lost it when the Japanese pushed us out of Asia.*) In Hawaii we were just one of the crowd and the local people knew that we didn't have much income. There wasn't much to do in town. Some of us took the island tour. This included the Mormon Temple, the Blowhole, and the upside-down falls. The next day we went out around town and out on the beach. The only hotel I remember was the Royal Hawaiian. We couldn't afford to go there, and actually, they did not want enlisted personnel in the hotel or on the beach behind it.

53

Leave Hawaii and Sail for the United States

The next day we sailed for San Francisco. It took seven days to go 2,200 miles. On the way a place was arranged for people to gamble. The ship's crew ran it and took a cut out of every pot. They couldn't lose. No one bothered the gamblers until the last night out. The master of arms and his crew busted up the game and took the money. One PFC refused to let them take his money. He was a redheaded Italian and wasn't afraid to assert himself. The master of arms let him keep the money but then decided to take the players up for captain's mast. I had not played until the last night. The captain appeared to be really mad and said that he would court-martial all of us, but there wouldn't be time, so he would get some work out of us. They put us in the spud locker to peel potatoes. That was where we were when we went under the Golden Gate Bridge and on up to Mare Island Navy Yard. We had been checking the dates as we were on the way from Hawaii and hoping to get back before the Fourth of July and have liberty in San Francisco. We made it back, but we didn't get liberty. We were assigned guard duty so the permanent personnel could have the day off.

54

Detained at Mare Island for Two Months

I thought I would be returned to the East Coast to be discharged, but I was held at Mare Island for two months and I got transferred then by getting furlough transfer, which meant paying my fare to Marine Barracks, Charleston Navy Yard, in South Carolina. Charleston was only two hundred miles from home. I shipped most of my gear home and traveled by train across country. It only took thirty-nine hours from Oakland to Chicago. I don't believe it's any better now. We stopped for a short time in Omaha. An army MP stopped me and wanted to know why I didn't have my tie tucked in. I told him that I was a U.S. Marine and that we didn't wear "ties," that I was wearing a "field scarf," and that they're not tucked in. He had probably never heard of the Marine Corps.

We picked up some army guys and they were soon in a blackjack game. A civilian was dealing. He caught me alone later and told me that he had been a marine for years, but now he was a civilian and worked in Reno as a card dealer. He told me to come back to the game and make small bets and he would pass the deal to me. The dealer usually wins. The percentage is in his favor. I took the deal and ended up quite a bit ahead. Old-timers from the Corps usually stuck together. After the game I changed into civilian clothes and moved up to the club car and relaxed with the people there. One woman was from South Carolina. I bought some drinks, but when she found out I was an enlisted person she wouldn't let me buy her any more drinks. We stayed together most of the way to Chicago. I had to lay over a few hours until I could catch a train south. (*At that time I felt safe anywhere in the United States. Fifty years later I was warned that it wasn't safe to take public transportation in Chicago.*) The train going south was not like the ones across country. It was slow and made a lot of stops. It took two days to get home.

55

Back Home from China—1941

It was late at night when I got to Belton, South Carolina, about six miles from home, but there was a stop nearer to home and the conductor agreed to let me off at a place called Dochino. I got my bag and started walking, but it was heavy, so I stopped at the first house that I came to and put the bag on the front porch. I didn't get dog-bitten or wake up the people in the house. It was easy walking then, and I would come back for the luggage later.

It was morning when I got to the farm. They were all up moving around. Things had changed. There were only four children still at home. They were expecting me, so there was no big surprise. I know they were happy to have me home, but they didn't make a big deal out of it, just shook hands and told me to get ready for breakfast. For breakfast we had country ham, eggs, and grits with hot biscuits and homemade molasses, not like what I had been having for a long time.

Mama had been having serious medical problems and had a kidney removed but had made a remarkable recovery. She kept on working and always stayed busy. (She lived another twenty-five years, and when she entered the Baptist Retirement Home she found plenty to do. She read to the blind residents and pushed wheelchairs for the ones who could not walk. She started up a group to make quilts and worked outside in the flower garden. She didn't like to see people sitting and doing nothing. Even when we were very young, she could find something for us to do. She would tell us to bring in wood for the stove or go to the well and get water. There was something to do all the time. She would have done well as a sergeant in the marines. After I retired, she would spend a few days with us on the farm and could always point out something that needed to be done.)

Later in the morning we got the '32 model Chevrolet out of the shed and went to pick up the baggage I had left the night before. I didn't like to ride with my father because he always stayed in the middle of the road. I expected him to have an accident. He started driving in his forties and never got very good at it. They said when he started to learn to drive he forgot how to stop the car and was saying, "Whoa, damn you." We picked up my bags, and I don't believe the folks in the house had noticed they were there. When we got back, Papa wanted to show me his cotton fields. The cotton was beginning to open and would soon be ready for picking. He only had a few acres because there was not much help. Mama never encouraged us to stay on the farm. My oldest brother was the only one who farmed for a living.

There was no electricity in our area when I first went away from home. In 1941 electricity came to our rural area, and this was probably the biggest thing that had happened in my lifetime. It meant that we could have lights, we had power to pump water, and we could have refrigerators and electric stoves and electric irons. My folks had enclosed a porch and put in plumbing. Each room had a single light bulb that you turned on and off by pulling a string. There were no wall switches. Most of the people put in plumbing as soon as they could afford it. My Uncle Alonzo said he didn't want a privy in his house. He kept using the one outdoors.

I had brought back a few things for the kids, and I gave them out after they got home from school. There were no expensive gifts, but they liked having something from China. I started checking up on people I knew before I left home. They had scattered. Some had found jobs and most of the ones my age were married. The few who had tried to make a living farming were not faring very well. Some had two or three kids and were sharecropping, which meant they only got to keep one-half of what they made.

The folks got a radio, and they really enjoyed it. They listened to *Lum and Abner, Amos and Andy,* and *Fibber McGee and Molly,* and they also liked gospel singing and preaching. The preachers always asked for money. I know my folks couldn't afford it, but they would send donations anyway. *I had not attended church for years except with my parents while I was on leave. I think these preachers just "got the call" and did not attend any colleges or seminaries. That was common in the poorer churches at that time. The pastor of our little Baptist church at that time had been having some problems, and some of the people wanted a change. One day at noon service he said that God wanted him to have a Cadillac, and this didn't go over very big. Most of the members didn't believe he was supposed to have an expensive car. They had old ones and a few members still came by horse and buggy. The Baptists don't have a rotation plan. Each church hired and fired the preacher. They called a meeting and voted to dismiss the preacher; over half voted to let him go. He refused to leave and said, "Brothers, I will stay here until hell freezes over." He had enough people on his side to keep paying his salary. He was splitting up the church, but I don't think that bothered him. Finally the deacons went to the Saluda Baptist Association and asked for help. They got him a smaller church, and he left without getting his Cadillac. He didn't last long at the new place and had to go to work to earn a living.*

56

Picking Cotton in South Carolina

The cotton was beginning to open up, and we made up some picking sacks and began to work. When I had left home I was determined to stay away from farming, but my help was needed and we stayed on the job until it was all picked. Times were changing, and we didn't have to haul the cotton to the gin with the mules and wagons. They came out with a truck and picked it up and carried it to the gin. They would buy it or bring the bales of cotton back. *You could hold it and hope the price would go up. We never waited. The money was needed to pay bills and buy some clothes for winter. If you didn't pay your bills you could ruin your credit and would be unable to buy fertilizer for the next year. It was fortunate that we grew just about everything to eat. Our menu didn't change, and our pants had patches on them.* My cousin ran a little country store about a mile away, and I would go there in the evenings. Most of them would be people I knew before I left home. Some of them would ask what I was doing and if I had found a job. They didn't know I had been anywhere.

My furlough was about up. I had walked around the neighborhood. I had picked muscadines that grew wild. They made good jam or jelly. The old collie and I had hunted squirrels. He was one of the best squirrel dogs I ever hunted with. I had plenty of time to think about my future but still had not made any definite plans. I knew I didn't want to farm or work in a factory, but I felt confident that I could manage. I had been on my own for over three years before I had enlisted in the Marine Corps.

57

Stationed in Charleston, South Carolina

I needed a ride to the naval base at Charleston, South Carolina. I had a cousin who was teaching school in the lower part of the state. She had managed to get through college in the middle of the depression, the only one of the children to make it. She had bought a new Ford, and she with a couple other young ladies drove me right up to the front gate. The marines on duty didn't look like the marines in the Fourth Regiment. Some of them were reserves who had been called up. Most of them had been in the regular Marine Corps, but some were not. Their uniforms would not have passed inspection at most other posts. Some were wearing civilian shoes. They checked me in and directed me to the barracks. It was Sunday and I reported to the first sergeant's office the next morning. He had been in World War I. The commanding officer had been called back from retirement. They didn't expect me to reenlist, so I was given odd jobs.

After I had been there about a week I was told to report to the first sergeant's office and would have to see the colonel. I had no idea what was going on. They had my service record out. The first sergeant carried me in to see the commanding officer. I stood at attention, and the colonel asked me why I had hit Mother Kelly over the head with a brick. Some marine had hit her, and they thought it might be me. I denied knowing anything about it. Mother Kelly ran a tough joint just a short way from the navy yard and had had problems before. I guess I convinced them I was not involved as they didn't check any further.

The company clerk was a PFC and had less than a year's service, but a vacancy for corporal came in and they gave it to him. I had passed the exam in China, and it was recorded in my service record. I still had not decided if I would reenlist, but I thought I had gotten a bad deal. I complained about it to the first sergeant. I asked him to check my record, and he looked and found it but wasn't going to do anything about it. I asked permission to see the colonel, and the sergeant refused. I grabbed my record and marched uninvited into the CO's office. I asked for permission to speak to him, and before he could refuse I placed my service record on his desk and asked him to look at it. I pointed out that I should have had the promotion instead of the company clerk. Instead of calling the MPs and having them arrest me, the CO agreed that I should have had the promotion. The first sergeant then said he would give me the next vacancy and would put me on the list for sergeant.

The navy opened an ammunition depot a few miles from Charleston, and some marines were sent up there for duty. A navy captain was in command, and a first sergeant was in charge. We stood watches at the main gate and had patrols in the area. The navy captain had a big house, and he kept sentries around it night and day. He had a marine for a driver of his car, and he used this driver to do personal things. The Captain liked to hunt ducks. He would come back and leave his boots with the first sergeant and tell him to have a marine clean them. Marines are not supposed to do this type of work, and the first sergeant resented it. He said, "I won't ask any of my men to do it. I'll do it myself." He was an outstanding marine.

58

Japanese Attack Pearl Harbor; United States Declares War

I was on liberty in downtown Charleston on December 7, 1941, when the Japanese attacked Pearl Harbor. I returned to barracks. Nobody knew what to do, and there were all kinds of rumors. Some thought they saw a submarine in the river. The next day the depot was officially opened. The name was the Goose Creek Naval Depot. I ran up the first flag, and then I went to Marine Barracks at Charleston and put in a request for duty overseas. *I was expecting to see the Marine Corps try to relieve the marines who had been caught in the Pacific. I didn't know how unprepared we were.*

59

Orders to Report to Dunedin,
Florida—December 1941

About a week after I put in my request for overseas duty I received orders to report to Dunedin, Florida, for training with amphibian tractors. *A man named Ruebling had made a vehicle for traveling through the swamps. The Marine Corps wanted to find out if these vehicles could be used for amphibious operations, and a small group had started working on this project in 1940. They took over the Dunedin Hotel for barracks and later had to pitch tents to take care of additional personnel.*

I picked up my orders and train ticket and left Charleston for Dunedin. On the way I got acquainted with some people going to Jackonsville. We were enjoying ourselves and when we got to Jacksonville they asked me to go with them, so I got my bag and rifle and went along. The next morning they carried me back to the railroad station. I would be a day late getting to Dunedin. I reported in and was told to report to the lobby of the hotel. I thought it was about being late, but that was never mentioned. They told me I was to be examined for promotion to sergeant. I told them that must be a mistake and that I had just arrived. My service record had arrived earlier. It wasn't much of an exam. They had already decided to promote me. I believe that one of the officers I had known in Quantico had seen my record and arranged for me to be promoted. *The Marine Corps was small before the war, and you would know a lot of*

151

people. There were only 17,000 people in the Corps when I enlisted in 1937. The Marine Corps would have 500,000 before the war ended.

We had liberty every other day. Everybody wanted to do something for the marines. They would give us a ride in any direction. It was only a short way to the nearest town of Clearwater. They all wanted to be helpful, so we were invited to various places. Once the Greek church in Tarpon Springs decided to have some of us up for a supper. About twelve people signed up to attend, but it was payday and they didn't make it, except for one private, and he arrived drunk. The colonel was upset by this and said that in the future anyone signing up for a dinner had better damn well attend and show up sober. We would not have gotten all this attention if we had been stationed at a base where they were accustomed to seeing troops.

60

I Meet My Future Wife in Clearwater, Florida

I was in Clearwater one night at a place called the Wonder Bar. It was the most popular café and bar in town. I was going to attend a dinner that was being put on by some group in town and wanted to get a girl to go with me. I saw some ladies sitting at the bar, and I walked over and asked if one of them would be interested in attending the event with me. Two of them were about my age and I expected one of them to go with me, but they wanted me to go with the younger girl. I thought she was about sixteen. She was wearing a turban and had a chipped front tooth. She was the prettiest girl I had seen. I found out that she was twenty years old, and at that time I was twenty-six. We went to the dinner but didn't stay long. I had been going out with different girls, but after I met Elaine I didn't go out with anyone else. I had had no interest in going steady or in getting married. I had seen too many people marry before they were eligible for family allowances. *As far as the Marine Corps was concerned, wives didn't exist if you were not a sergeant or above. Married couples had to scrimp to get by and usually had a rough time finding a place to live, and there were not many jobs near the bases. The married men were different from the single men. They didn't want to be away from their wives, and when they had children it was even worse. A married marine couldn't reenlist if he was not a first sergeant or staff NCO. They used to say, "If the*

153

Marine Corps wanted you to have a wife they would have issued one for you." A lot of the marriages failed. You were expected to put the Marine Corps ahead of everything else. Several years later, I heard a black colonel being interviewed and they asked him if he had problems with being black in the Marine Corps and he said, "No." The interviewer asked him why he thought this was so, and he answered, "It's simple. In the Marine Corps they treat everyone like they are black."

61

Training with Amphibian Tractors

I kept on training with the amphibian tractors. We would go out to an island and test them. There were lots of bugs to be worked out. We had problems with the tracks coming off. They were new and it took time to get them ready for combat operations. Once they carried us to Lakeland and to Ford Machinery, a plant where they built these tractors. We met some of the people who were building them, and they met some of the marines who would operate them from Guadalcanal to Okinawa, over a period of one and one-half years. *If we had landed in Japan in 1945 there would have been six battalions, one to each division.*

62

Orders to San Diego, Promotion to Platoon Sergeant, Elaine and I Are Married

In April we got orders to go to San Diego and I expected to get orders for overseas. Elaine and I had not made any definite plans. She came to the railway station to say good-bye. There were lots of families and friends to see us off. We had a good trip on a Pullman and made the trip in six days. Soon after we got to California I was promoted to platoon sergeant, and this would allow me to be eligible for married allowances! This was a big day in my life, and I wrote a letter to Elaine and asked her to marry me. *The Battalion left without me, as I was still expecting to go overseas but first had to attend first sergeant school.*

After Elaine arrived, we learned it was necessary to have blood tests and wait three days before we could be married, so we got on the bus and went to Yuma, Arizona, where there was no waiting period. There were lots of people in line to get married. It was midnight before our turn came. I didn't have a ring, and this just about floored the justice of the peace. He would start to say, "With this ring I thee wed," but there was no ring! Someone asked the girl who had just gotten married if we could borrow her ring. She was angry and said, "No, I will never take it off." We were finally married without a ring.

The temperature at midnight was over one hundred degrees. We rode the bus back to San Diego, and I stood up all the way back. We had rented a place in Old Town, San Diego. It was Sunday and I didn't have to report in until Monday morning. I had not asked for any days off, though I feel sure I could have gotten two or three days off. I thought they couldn't get by without me. We were married August 16, 1942, and I didn't ship out until the following March. It was fortunate that we had this time together, because it was two years and three months before I got back.

My company had gone overseas, so I was transferred to another outfit that was several miles out from where we were staying. We didn't have a car, but I managed to get rides or take the bus. Elaine took a job delivering food to the workers at the aircraft plant, and this enabled us to get by. We had to move around to find a place to live, but about two months before I went overseas we got a little house in an avocado grove, just a short ways out.

Jack and Elaine Wright on honeymoon in Old Town, San Diego, 1942

63

Ten-Day Leave to Visit Family in South Carolina

I knew that I would be going overseas, and I got a ten-day leave and started out for South Carolina. I traveled on military aircraft and several times had to wait. I got as far as Saint Louis and had to ride the train to Atlanta. When I arrived in Atlanta there were ladies looking out for service people. They would drive us wherever we needed to go. I was driven to the bus station and got a ticket for the rest of the way. I thought that was nice of the ladies to help travelers out. It was wartime and almost everyone was patriotic and wanted to help. I got to Anderson, South Carolina, and took a cab for a few remaining miles to home. By now all the family had left home except my youngest sister, who was about fifteen years old. I only stayed a few days. *One brother was working as a carpenter in Greenville, South Carolina, where they were building barracks at an air base. He was paid ninety dollars per week. I had never known anyone to make that much money, but he was working sixty hours a week.* At the air base I started looking for a ride back to San Diego. I did get a ride, but it wasn't going very far. It took about twenty-four hours, and I had to wait a time or two. I got to Las Vegas about daylight and everything was open, but I didn't stay long. It was only about two hundred miles to San Diego, and I decided to hitchhike the rest of the way. I got back before night.

64

Back in San Diego, Orders for Overseas, Elaine Goes to Ohio

The next morning I reported in and found that we had orders for overseas. We started getting our gear ready to go. I had told Elaine that we were about ready to ship out, and she was making plans to go to Ohio to stay with her folks.

They didn't let anyone know where we were going, but taxi drivers and waitresses kept saying that we were going to Auckland, New Zealand. I don't know where they got their information, but they were right. I had always looked forward to going to new places, but this time was different. I was leaving my wife and didn't know when or if I would return, but I wanted to have a part in the war. If I wanted to stay in the service I thought it would be better to have wartime duty in my record. It turned out that wouldn't have any bearing unless you got one of the important decorations.

*   *   *

Part IX

65

March 1943—Off to the War, First Stop New Zealand

We left on a Dutch ship. Before the war she had been a passenger ship. The crew was Dutch and Javanese. The Javanese were small, dark people and very polite. When they wanted to pass you they would say, "Gangway, please." The ship was carrying more people than it should have. The decks were crowded and living conditions were very bad. There were only two meals per day and a lot of time standing in line. Since I had been promoted I had good accommodations, not as good as the officers, but better than I had before. We didn't have an escort, and it took seventeen days to get to New Zealand. The CO of troops was a colonel. He had been a lieutenant colonel in Shanghai when I was there. He had the reputation of being a nitpicker and an oddball, and he had not changed. He had a big ugly bulldog that he had brought aboard. He had one marine detailed to take care of the dog. He would feed steaks to the dog while the men were making out with very poor fare. I was surprised that someone didn't throw the animal over the side. The ship was blacked out after dark, but you could stay out on deck if you wanted.

When we got to Auckland we tied up in town. It was at night and we didn't offload until morning. A few of us went ashore to look around and see if we could find a drink. It was too late and the pubs had closed, but we were approached by one of the local citizens, who told us that if we wanted a drink we would have to see a "slygroger." That is what we called bootlegger. After a while slygroger did come around and said he could get us drinks, but it would cost a couple of pounds. We didn't have any pounds, but he accepted dollars and took off. He didn't come back and we decided that the local people weren't to be trusted 100 percent. Most of the people were honest and glad to see us.

The Japanese were only a few hundred miles away. The Auckland men were fighting in North Africa. A reinforced Japanese division could have taken over the entire country.

We started moving the following morning. Just outside of Auckland at a race track we pitched tents and got settled in. It was in April, which is fall in New Zealand. We trained almost every day. Everything stayed damp. I was sharing a tent with an NCO who snored. He would shake the tent when he let go. We got the company located and were cleaning up the area.

We had a young marine who had been promoted to sergeant, and I assigned him duty as police sergeant. He was told to get the troops out and clean up around the place. He stayed alone for a little while. Then he came back and said he couldn't get them to do anything, that they wouldn't come out of their tents. I told him that if he could not get them to work he should not be a sergeant. He had been very proud of his sergeant stripes and had probably told his girlfriend about them. He went back and this time he got the troops out. You could hear him yelling and swearing all over camp. He had learned that you can't always be a nice guy.

The mail had to be censored by officers, and they were not supposed to repeat anything they read. One day one of our officers was censoring the mail. The writer of one particular letter had a lot of gripes. He didn't like anything about the setup, and he especially didn't like the first sergeant. The officer thought that was funny since I was the one he was complaining about but read further and the writer said that the damn officers were no better. The officer didn't think that was funny, and he said to get that man in here. I don't know what the officer said to him, but I guess the writer started censoring his own mail before he turned it over for censorship. One man wrote a letter home and said: "As I have nothing to do, I am writing, and as I have nothing to say, I am closing."

The company commander had not been in the service before the war. He had probably had managerial experience in civilian life, but the Marine Corps was different. He let a warrant officer advise him on how to run the company. One day the WO told the captain that he wanted to handle the liberty for the men. Fifty percent had to stay in camp. It didn't make any difference who went on liberty as long as half of the company was available for duty. The reason the WO wanted to handle the liberty was because one of the NCOs had come back in service and was overage except for duty in the States. He had managed to get a waiver to allow him to serve overseas. He was a widower and was going with a New Zealand woman, and he would go out every night if he could. This one officer didn't like this man, so he told the company commander that he wanted to run the liberty list. The CO agreed and told me to turn it over to this officer. I told him that as first sergeant I was supposed to be in charge of the liberty list. I told him if he wanted someone else to be first sergeant he didn't need me. I walked out of the office and went to see the sergeant major at regimental headquarters and asked him to transfer me to another company. That is not the acceptable way to do things, and in peace time I would have been court-martialed, but times

165

had changed and I was transferred to the amphibian tractor battalion.

I knew most of the officers and NCOs, and I was glad to be back in the battalion. We didn't get to see much of the country, but before leaving we took a train ride to Rotorura. We spent the day with the natives at the park. At that time they lived on a reservation. We were entertained by their singing and dancing. Some of their men had been wounded in North Africa and were back recuperating. Some were in bad shape, but I know they were glad to be back in New Zealand. The natives sang several songs, but their favorite was "You Are My Sunshine." We returned on the train. The trains were all old, something like the trains we had at home several years earlier. I liked the country and the people and wish I could have returned after the war.

66

Leave for the Solomons—July 1943

We left for the Solomons about the first of July. July is in the middle of their winter, but it wasn't cold, just damp and disagreeable weather. We moved aboard ship, but we didn't leave that day. We were allowed to go to Auckland but we were supposed to have uniforms to wear. Before we left camp we were told to turn in our uniforms for storage. The ones who kept their uniforms were going ashore, and the ones who had followed orders were confined to the ship. This really upset a lot of people. One old-timer requested permission to see the CO. The CO saw the unfairness and put out the word that people could go in town in their utility clothing. *The old sergeant had a long name that started with a A and ended with a Z, so people called him A to Z, or Azee. He had retired before the war and was called back. He was over fifty years old and wasn't supposed to go overseas. He must have known someone and had managed to get a waiver to go overseas. He had been in World War I and had served in the Russian army. He had an accent and when he heard people complaining he would say, "It could be a thousand times vorser." He was impressed by some of the Russian generals. He liked one general named Timo 'shanko, but the other sergeants kidded him and said, "Tim O'Shanko is an Irishman." A to Z stayed overseas and was in Bougainville, but after that I think he realized he was too old and he agreed to return to the States. He retired again and went to Florida and lived several more years.*

67

Welcomed to Guadalcanal by Tokyo Rose

We got near Guadalcanal and had a submarine alert. Everyone not on duty topside had to stay below with the hatches closed. *Later in the war the policy changed. You had a choice so that you could stay topside if you wanted to, but the compartments were closed. I always stayed outside.* We reached the beach late in the afternoon and didn't have most of the gear ashore. I insisted on getting up a cover. I told the others that it always rained at night in the tropics. It didn't rain a drop. I was reminded of my forecast a few times. The communication section set up a longwave radio, and we were welcomed to Guadalcanal by Tokyo Rose. She predicted that all kinds of bad things were going to happen to us. I don't know how she got her information, but she knew we were the Third Marine Division and that headquarters was located in a large coconut grove. The island had been declared secured a few weeks. Before we arrived there were a few stragglers about, but they were not a problem. We had enemy planes at times, mostly nuisance flights. Marine Aviation had that part of the Solomons pretty well under control, but the Japanese had managed to hold onto the islands west of where we were.

There had been lots of bloody fighting after the marines landed in August 1942. It was probably the first time the Japanese had been stopped anywhere. They had taken Formosa and Korea several years before. In the 1930s they had occupied Manchuria and they had controlled most of China.

68

Combat in Bougainville—November 1943

Our first operation was on the island of Bougainville. We landed in November 1943. It was a miserable place. After you got inland a few hundred yards you ran into a swamp that no tanks or wheels could get through. The amphibian tracks had been built for places like that, and for a few weeks we moved everything. Supplies were moved up, and the wounded were brought back. One day the commanding general of the division was at the front and started back to the beach. He hailed the driver of an amphibian tractor and asked for a ride through the swamp. The driver refused and said he had orders not to pick up anyone except the wounded. General Turnage said, ''All right,' and started wading back through the swamp. I had known him in Quantico and China. He was an officer and a gentleman, and I'm sorry that he didn't finish up as commandant of the Marine Corps.

A couple of nights after we landed, a large number of Japanese planes came and dropped bombs. One of our companies was hit and lost about a dozen men and several more were wounded. I was in a shallow foxhole several yards away, more afraid than I ever was before or since. I tried to crawl under my helmet, and I cursed all Japs everywhere. Maybe it was because I was wet and tired and needed sleep. The next time the planes came, I was dry and had consumed some coffee and I didn't even get in a hole. One time an

LST pulled up to shore and lowered the ramp. Sailors came ashore looking for souvenirs, and marines went aboard scrounging. A plane came in and the alarm sounded. Sailors ran back to the ship, and the marines headed to shore. To each his own.

The Seabees had performed a miracle by building an airstrip in just a few days. Our planes started operating and we didn't have any large-scale attacks. After the Seabees built the airstrip they dug up coral and built a road across the swamp and then all the vehicles could go through. After the road was completed the Seabees put up a sign that read: "When the Marines get to heaven with their caps at a jaunty tilt, they will travel on roads that the Seabees built." They were entitled to boast a little. They always did outstanding work.

69

Return to Guadalcanal on Christmas Eve, 1943

Just a short while before Christmas the army moved a division in and we got ready to return to Guadalcanal. We had left part of the battalion behind. Camp was ready to move back into. We returned on Christmas Eve. It wasn't like the States, but a generator was furnishing power for lights and we could have a shower bath. A large drum was placed on poles and filled with water. The sun heated the water, and it was the first real bath we had had for two months. We had been washing in the ocean whenever we could or in streams of fresh water. We didn't have haircuts during this time. Some had beards, and no one had been able to wash clothes during all this time. We must have smelled bad. But the men felt like they had done their jobs well and that now they were veterans. We had been living mostly on rationing. Now we had hot food and a place to sit down and eat. It was the same stuff we had always complained about: no fresh meat or vegetables. We had mostly dehydrated potatoes, powdered eggs, and milk. The only meat was Spam and occasionally some mutton from Australia or New Zealand. The troops called it goat meat. It wasn't very good, but the tents were dry and we slept on cots. It was a lot better than sleeping on the ground, and we weren't getting shot at. I don't know how they managed it, but we had turkey and the trimmings for Christmas dinner.

Soon after we got back a vacancy came up for sergeant major. I was the senior first sergeant, and I was offered the promotion. It wasn't a pay increase and I was satisfied as company first sergeant but all promotions had been temporary and I wanted to stay in. I expected the Marine Corps would reduce most of us back a pay grade or more after the war. *I knew the battalion commander and I would be in battalion headquarters. He had no active service before the war, and he didn't like people who had been in before the war because he knew he didn't measure up very well with the career officers. He had a reserve commission, but he wanted to stay in after the war. He spent most of his time trying to cultivate the right people. He had very little concern about the men, but he had some good people in battalion headquarters and they were good at their jobs. On Bougainville he stayed in his hole. But the battalion did a good job and he got the credit. One day he burned his hand while washing his mess gear, and he got the Purple Heart for that. This ribbon was supposed to be for wounds received in action.*

This colonel got a PFC to be his orderly. He had the private cleaning up his tent and doing his laundry. The troops gave the PFC a hard time. They would holler at him in the chow line and ask if he got all the dingleberries out of the colonel's drawers. He wanted out of this job, and he didn't know what to do. He asked me if he had to work for the CO. I got the Marine Corps manual out and showed him an article that said a marine was not required to be a servant. He quoted this to the colonel and was relieved. This took a lot of nerve, but the CO didn't have much choice. The manual was the Marine Corps Bible.

70

Amtracs to Emiran

After we had been back a couple of months we got orders to send a company of amphibian tractors to a place called Emiran. I think hardly anyone had ever heard of it. It was beyond Bougainville and near Rabaul. We expected to be attacked by Japanese aircraft, but we didn't see a single plane. We anchored out a few hundred yards and launched the amphibian tractors. We were to land a company of marine raiders. These people had seen more combat than most outfits. I wasn't supposed to make the landing, but one platoon didn't have an officer, so he told me to take the troops in. When we got near the shore somebody fired a round and everybody started firing. After we got ashore a native came out waving a white cloth and asking us to stop firing. He said there were not any Japanese on the island and had not been for two months. We didn't hang around long, but a group moved in and started an airstrip. *The island was small and the airfield would take up most of it. It was farther west than we had been before, but no enemy planes came out to attack our convoy. A few months earlier it would have been impossible to operate in this area.*

71

Move North to the Marianas

Soon after we returned we got ready to move north to the Marianas. *I had stopped at Guam while going and returning from China. It wasn't exactly an island paradise but would be better than Guadalcanal.* This time I was to stay in the rear with the gear. A major was in charge, and I was the senior enlisted man. We had about one hundred enlisted men and a lot of equipment. I would have preferred to go with the battalion for the landing, but the personnel sergeant major had missed Bougainville and was determined to make the coming operation.

72

Orders to Go to Guam—but First Layover in the Marshalls

A few weeks later we had orders to board ship and join the rest of the battalion at Guam. There had been delays in securing the island, so we laid over in the Marshalls for several days. There were ships there as far as you could see, and for the first time since we had been overseas they were lighted up at night. We finally got orders to move on to Guam and we landed after the operation was officially over, but there were lots of stragglers. The commanding general let the men go after them, but they wouldn't surrender and had to be killed. Most of them committed suicide. Occasionally a group would get together for a banzai attack and would be killed by the marines or blow themselves up with a hand grenade.

Our battalion had been lucky. Only a few people had been killed or wounded. As support troops they were not required to assault the beaches, but they were exposed to enemy fire when transporting troops and supplies. The town of Agana was flattened. About the only thing I could recognize was the bandstand in the center of the town. Most of the natives had survived. I got to know some of them. They told me about the navy petty officer who had hidden out all during the war. His name was Tweed and he was considered something of a hero. The people I talked to wouldn't criticize him, but he caused some of them to be beaten and a few were killed because they wouldn't tell the Japanese where he was hiding.

Living conditions on Guam were much better than what we had had on Guadalcanal. We got a little better food and everybody had a club card and we were allowed a couple of beers per week. The staff NCOs got the Seabees to put up a Quonset hut, and we managed to get tables and chairs. It was quite comfortable. *The camp was named after Captain Mills, who was killed during the landing. He was from Tupelo, Mississippi. He was a reserve officer, but he liked the Corps and would probably have stayed in the military if he had survived the war. He was my company commander on Bougainville. The colonel gave out ribbons to all the officers except a couple. I don't think most of them had done anything extraordinary. The ones left out had probably done something to make him mad. The battalion adjutant said the colonel had a hole so deep that he was almost AWOL. He stayed in this night and day, but he still got a decoration.*

The battalion doctor was a naval reserve officer and cared nothing about a military career. He was picked up one night by the MPs. He didn't have any insignia on his shirt and had had a few drinks. The MPs asked him who he was, and he replied, "I am the quack from the Amph Tracs." He had a good sense of humor.

*   *   *

176

Part X

73

Combat in the Pacific—1945

About the middle of February 1945 we loaded up the amphibian tractors and headed north. This operation would be nearer Japan than any ground forces had been, only about six hundred miles from mainland Japan. The name of the place was Iwo Jima, a small island that very few people had ever heard of before this time.

We stopped at Saipan the first night. It had been secured the previous summer. I knew a lot of people in the Second Amph Trac Battalion and took the opportunity to visit with them. They were located on the beach and pretty well settled in. They had an all-night poker game going on, and I joined them for a while. They were cutting the pot and using the money to buy whiskey from the pilots who were bringing it in. They were charging sixty dollars per bottle, a lot of money at that time, but there wasn't anything else to buy. A few of us left the game and went for a swim.

74

Learning the Truth about Tarawa

We stayed up all night talking, and I found out some of the terrible things that had happened in the battle for Tarawa. The first wave of marines came in on amtracs. Just about everything went wrong, and they were exposed to fire as they struggled to reach land and hundreds of marines were killed or wounded. The second landing had it even worse. There were not enough LTVs to go around, and they had to debark from regular landing craft and wade across the reefs. We learned later that the marines had suffered 3,000 casualties, including a battalion commander, on an atoll that was barely a speck on a map. This battalion had not been scheduled to make the Iwo operations but had been planning to go to Okinawa in April.

75

The Battle of Iwo Jima

The next morning I returned to the LST, and that afternoon we sailed for Iwo. We arrived in the morning while it was still dark. Ships of all descriptions were shelling the beaches. I don't think so many ships were ever together again unless it was at Okinawa. A cruiser near us was firing on Mount Surabachi. There was a large tunnel that went far back into the mountain. The cruiser was firing into the opening, and we could see shells go out of sight and then they fired directly above the tunnel. They were trying to seal the tunnel by knocking dirt on the entrance. This was very impressive, but it was discovered later that the Japanese were so well dug in that most of them survived all bombardment. They had cement bunkers several feet thick and covered with sand. They would have to be attacked by men using flame throwers and hand grenades, and this resulted in a large loss of the attackers. There was no cover and they had to proceed out in the open and uphill.

A Congressional Medal of Honor marine sergeant, John Basilone, was killed while he was going up the first hill. He was not supposed to go into combat again after he had won the Medal of Honor at Guadalcanal, but he insisted. This landing operation was not like any of the previous landings. The general didn't believe in banzai attacks, and he made us pay for his misjudgment every step of the way. The Japanese would stage attacks where hundreds, and in some cases thousands, of screaming men charged

181

into the battle area. Only a few prisoners would be taken. We were support troops and not supposed to take part in the assault, but we were exposed to enemy fire and some of the men operating the vehicles were lost. Wheeled vehicles could not make it through the deep volcanic sand, and for a couple of days we moved most of the supplies. Later they laid down marston matting, and amphibious trucks could make it up the hill.

There was a lot of confusion because of the loss of officers and senior NCOs. Sometimes a company would be led by a sergeant and have only a handful of men left. But even without leaders the men kept climbing up the hill.

The adjutant and I came ashore in midmorning. The first day, our men were assigned to the battalions to transport troops and supplies and we had to get the wounded out to the hospital ship. There wasn't much we could do. All the beaches were under direct fire. We started to dig a hole, which was difficult because the sand kept sliding into the hole. Three of us covered up with a shelter half. I don't think we slept much, and it felt cold. It was probably about fifty degrees, but we had been in the tropics for several months and this was quite a change. We didn't eat anything the first day, but the next morning we found some rations. They had changed to a ration called ten-in-one. This included bacon and we had not had bacon since we left New Zealand. We made a good fire by putting sand in a can and adding gasoline. Smelling the aroma of the sizzling bacon was almost as good as eating it.

The second day, we improved our hole by lining it with sandbags to keep it from caving in. This was going to be our home for a couple of months. *Last year, I talked to the officer I had shared the hole with and asked him how long we were on the island. He said we were there sixty-two days. I thought it had been two or three weeks.*

We were near Mount Suribachi, and on the third day we looked up and saw some of our troops advancing to the top of the mountain. We were watching when they ran up the first flag. Later they ran up a second flag so they could get better pictures. I never thought much about how much publicity would follow. At that time we still had several weeks before the island would be secured. The secretary of the navy, James Forrestal, came ashore with the general. The general's name was Holland Smith, but he was called Howlin' Mad Smith. I don't know how he came to be called that. The army was very displeased with him at that time because he had relieved an army division commander on Saipan. During the operation the going was slow and we were losing a lot of troops. A reporter asked General Smith if he was going to be able to take Iwo. He replied, "We will take it if it takes every man we've got." It would have been humiliating to let the Japanese push us back into the ocean. The operation dragged on. We were pushing them toward the far end of the island and had secured the airport. A plane came in with some kind of engine trouble. They had been bombing Japan, and I guess they thought they couldn't make it back to Guam. A couple of us started to go up to take a look and were caught out in the open when the Japanese started shelling the field. There was no place to go, but we escaped unharmed. After that I stayed away from the airfield. Later on planes could land, and planes that were in trouble did land. A large number of planes and their crews were saved. If we had landed in Japan, planes from Iwo would have been used to support the landing. (*In 1952 I was flying to Korea and when we approached Iwo the pilot asked if anyone wanted to take a closer look. We all did, so he dropped down low and circled the island. It looked entirely different from the air.*)

76

We Leave Iwo—April 1945

We left Iwo about the last week of April 1945. We had been there since the nineteenth of February. We boarded a troopship with just our weapons. The amtrac vehicles were left behind. Anyway, they were about worn out. We would get new equipment when we got to Hawaii.

We stopped at Guam. Some of the battalion were still there, but some had already left for Maui. We stayed up all night. We went back to board the ship, but it was already moving. They saw us and lowered the ladder, and we climbed up on the deck. I don't know what would have happened if we had failed to get aboard. The ship we were on was prepared to haul troops from Iwo, but since we had lost so many people we only had about half as many as was expected. I had looked forward to some decent food, but my stomach had shrunk and I could only eat small amounts. The thing I liked best was toast, but after a few days I was back to normal.

77

On the Beach at Maui

We crossed the International Date Line on Easter Sunday. We regained the day we had lost going out, so we had two Easters coming back. We landed on Maui and camped in what had been a sugarcane field not far from Lahaina. As usual, we were on the beach. It was a good location, and the weather was pleasant. We were allowed liberty but had to rotate days to keep from overcrowding the few towns on Maui. I always went to Lahaina. It was nearer and still looked a lot like it did in the earlier times. After we had been there a couple of weeks some of the men started rotating back to the United States. They were keeping some of us back. We were to remain and prepare for the landing in Japan in the fall.

Change of Plans—Accepted for OCS Program

It looked like I would stay overseas a while longer, but a letter came asking people to go to OCS in Quantico, Virginia, and I was accepted for the program. *Earlier in the war I could have had a commission as a second lieutenant, but it would have been in the reserves and an old-timer advised me that after the war I could be put on the inactive list. I was satisfied to be an enlisted man. I also expected everyone to be reduced in rank when the war was over. All promotions had been temporary since 1941, and I had decided to stay in the service. After the war I would have nine years when my second enlistment expired.*

78

Return to USA

My orders were to go to the airfield at Guam and fly to the United States, but when I reported in I was told that my orders had been changed and I would return to the United States on a British aircraft carrier that was going to San Diego. I boarded the ship and was assigned quarters in the chief's compartment. There were no planes aboard, and we had the whole topside open. About midway the ship received the news that the war in Europe was over. They took the news calmly. There was no shouting or firing of guns, but they ordered an extra ration of rum for all hands.

I reported with my orders to the marine recruit depot in San Diego. I expected to leave in a day or two, but they kept me about a week and then they told me I would be in charge of a group going to Chicago. We were to travel by train, but it was not on a Pullman. They had rigged up several bunks to each car. They were known as cattle cars, but the food was good and everyone was excited after being away from home for two years or more. When we got to Saint Louis a group of ladies met us at the train and invited us to a luncheon in a large hotel. I don't know how they knew we were coming and that we would have a six-hour layover, but we had a fine time and lots of good food. When we got to Chicago I passed the orders out to the men. After that, I could travel on my own to Cleveland, Ohio, where my wife was waiting.

79

Elaine and I on Vacation Together at Last

My wife and I had not seen each other for two years and three months, but fortunately, we did have six months together before I went overseas, so we didn't feel like complete strangers. The next day we rode the train to her hometown, Conneaut, Ohio. I had never met any of her folks, but we got along fine. Elaine and I did not own a car, so we started looking for one. All of the dealers wanted us to have something to trade in or "money under the table." No cars had been made during the war. We found a 1941 model for about twice what it had cost before the war, but we needed transportation. My brother and his wife and little girl came from Detroit and rode with us to South Carolina. I had never met his wife and child and had not seen him since 1938. Gasoline was rationed, but I got enough cards for the entire trip. They were pretty liberal with people returning from overseas. It took two days to make the trip.

The following weekend, my family gathered for a reunion at the home place. There was lots of food, and many relatives came. We stayed home for a few days and then drove to Quantico, Virginia.

80

Report to OCS in Quantico, Virginia, but Did Not Stay in the Program, New Orders for Camp Pendleton, California

We checked in, but the place was crowded and there was no place to rent. We got a motel room a few miles away, and I reported to candidate class. We were told that we would stay in the barracks. I wanted to be with my wife, but it was beginning to seem like a boot camp again. When we had the first formation a staff sergeant picked the three most senior NCOs and told us to start cleaning up the "head"—military slang for toilets.

We immediately broke ranks and walked into the colonel's office and told him we wanted out of the program. He agreed and we went to marine headquarters in Washington, D.C., and asked for assignments. I got Camp Pendleton, California. The orders came down through channels.

My wife and I started driving across country. We both liked Southern California and knew people around San Diego. It was hard to find a place to live, but we lived in a motel nearby for a while and then we got in government housing near the base.

81

War Ends in August 1945; I Am in the United States for a Year and Then Back to China (1946)

I was expecting to go back overseas, but the war ended in August. I got a job mustering people out of the service. Almost everyone who was eligible for discharge wanted out. We worked seven days and didn't shut down for Christmas.

Everything slowed down in the spring and I put in for leave, but the day my leave was supposed to start I got orders for China. I had been in the United States for about a year. I had always looked forward to getting orders and moving on to new places, but it wasn't the same after I was married. My wife went back to her folks' home in Ohio, and I sailed back to the Orient.

82

It Took Seventeen Days to Reach Tsingtao

We didn't stop anywhere on the way. It took seventeen days to reach Tsingtao. On the way we passed through some mines that had drifted out from some island. We slowed speed, and the navy tried to explode them with machine-gun fire. They were not hitting the mines. A marine WO picked up a rifle and started hitting them right away. It was a good trip and no rough weather. I was billeted in the chief's quarters, and the food was good. It wasn't like the *Chaumont* or *Henderson*. We got off the ship and I saw two people at the dock who had been on the dock in Shanghai in 1939. Everything had changed. Very few of the men had been in before the war. Things were unsettled, and communists were around the countryside. Sometimes there would be firing at night in the city, but it was random and I never heard of anyone getting shot. Curfew was at eleven o'clock.

We older NCOs who had been in China previously liked Chinese food, but the younger folks wanted strictly American. We would pool our money and have the cook prepare a dinner for us about once a week. A Chinaman took a few of us who had been in China in the thirties out for a banquet that lasted about four hours. When we thought we had finished our dinner he asked what we liked most, and when we told him he ordered another full plate of it. His object was to get us to ship out some goods for him to sell. One thing he was interested in was old tires. He was going to make shoes out of them. He would have liked for some of us to work full-time exporting goods to him from the United States. A few months later the communists took over and I imagine he was put out of business.

We had a staff NCO club, and one sergeant brought a Japanese woman. He was criticized by some of the marines, but he said he wasn't fighting the women and he kept on seeing her.

Marines had a habit of picking up pets. They had parrots, dogs, and a monkey. One man had adopted a goat and people complained, but he didn't listen. One night when he wasn't around we opened the door of the compound and pushed the goat out into the street. He didn't get far. He bleated one time and I guess he was the entrée for a few hungry Chinese.

One battalion commander thought he would set an example cleaning up the area. He had marines out cleaning the streets. The Chinese laughed and pointed their fingers and said, "Marines all same as coolies." After that the marines let the Chinese do the coolie jobs. Some of the oldtimers had had several tours of duty in China. They had been in Tientsen, Peking, and Shanghai. They could stay two and one-half years, and then they would have to go back to the States. But as soon as they reenlisted they would put in for China duty. Some had Chinese women they lived with. One marine had a woman from Hong Kong. She spoke English with a British accent. He had left her in Shanghai when he went back to the United States, but she joined him in Tsingtao after the war. I asked him how he managed to make contact with her, and he said his room boy located her and got them together.

We had tropical hours. This means we started the day early and secured at one o'clock in the afternoon. The marines had taken over the golf course, and I started playing in the afternoons. It was a nine-hole course and we didn't take the game seriously, but I continued to play after I returned to the United States. Those of us who were married wanted our wives to join us in Tsingtao. One day they got the married staff NCOs together and told us we could put in to have our dependents join us. The next day they said we couldn't, but that we could go back to the United States or go to Peking with our dependents.

83

Return to U.S.

I decided to return to the United States. I wanted to have some time with my wife. We had only had one anniversary together during our first four years of marriage.

A lieutenant, another first sergeant, and I were assigned the job of bringing back a large group of men who were going to be separated from the service and all of the battalion's gear. A colonel was troop commander, but he said not to bother him unless it was an emergency. He had to sign for some messages a few times, but we had to see to the troops and the battalion's equipment. We ran into a typhoon when we were going by Japan. It lasted about four days. Most of the men got very sick. They were belowdecks and in their bunks most of the time. They had to hold onto something secure if they wanted to eat, and after a couple of days they didn't come out on deck at all. They simply refused to move. I took a few of the NCOs who weren't sick and got clubs and chased them out into the fresh air. They improved right away. I think they were so mad they forgot about being sick. They were a pretty good group, and all they wanted to do was to get home and get discharged. Some of them had been drafted and were not interested in staying in any longer than they had to. When we got to San Diego they went to Camp Pendleton to get separated from the service. That left three of us to get the gear unloaded and into storage. I had brought back quite a bit of items and had them crated, marked: OFFICE GEAR, and then loaded into a truck and put in a compartment belowdecks. The hatches were closed, but there was a small entrance that sailors used, and much to my disappointment they took everything except two rugs. There was nothing I could do about it.

84

Elaine and I Buy a Red Convertible and Travel

After we got things in storage we were able to spend time with our families. My wife and I bought a red convertible with a white top and spent weekends traveling around Southern California. One time we took a week off and went to the northern part of the state. We were in civilian clothes and we thought people would think we were rich tourists, but everywhere we stopped people wanted to know if we were looking for work. I had worked in a gold mine and had panned for gold in Siskiyou County up near the Oregon border ten years before. I wanted my wife to see this place where I had been. It seemed as if nothing had changed. The little town looked like it did when I was there before, and there was sort of a road up to the mine. The two people who were panning for gold were still there. One had sunk shafts back into a mountain and was digging out ore. He was hoping to hit a vein that had played out. Elaine and I had lunch with him and he seemed really pleased to have a good-looking young woman helping him in his kitchen. I don't believe that he had ever been married.

Elaine and I came back to San Francisco and stayed a couple of days at the Marine Memorial Hotel. We were right in the heart of town. We could walk to places or ride the cable cars. We ate at the Fisherman's Wharf and had some excellent Chinese food. We had a nice trip down the coast on the way back. At last we had decent housing after living in trailers and Quonset huts.

I was first sergeant of an amphibian tractor company. My company commander was a man I had known when he was a sergeant in China. He had been commissioned and was now a major. He had been married to a Russian woman, and she had been left behind during the war. He found her in Peking after the war and managed to get her to the States.

85

Orders to Parris Island, South Carolina

Everything was fine, but I had been away from home most of the time and decided to request transfer to Charleston or Parris Island, South Carolina. I got orders for Parris Island. I had accumulated four months of unused leave. I could get paid for two months but would have to take the rest or lose it. Elaine and I got in our convertible and headed east. We traveled light in those days. Most of our belongings were carried in our car. We stayed on the farm for a couple of weeks and then went to Detroit to visit two of my brothers. From there we went to my wife's family in Conneaut, Ohio. We stayed a few days and then went back to South Carolina. We still had lots of leave time left, so we took off to Florida and visited some cousins. It rained all the time we were there, and after that we went back to see our folks. We still had a week's leave and I would lose it if I didn't take it, but I decided to check in early.

I had not been back to Parris Island since I left boot camp, but I was returning as a sergeant major. There were too many senior NCOs, but I got assigned first sergeant of the casual company. I had troops of all kinds, some of them awaiting discharge for various reasons. One recruit's mother opted to follow him around the drill field watching her son while he was training. The CO got fed up and turned him over to casual company for discharge. The company had a dozen or so men whose jobs were to deliver the remains of the bodies that were shipped back. They were gone most of the time but had to check into casual company when they were not delivering bodies. Some of them were officers who had reverted back to enlisted status. I had one man who was awaiting discharge for fraudulent enlistment. He had a police record and had used his brother's birth certificate to enlist. There was usually a few day's delay in processing the papers, and they were assigned jobs cleaning up the area. One man came in the office and said he wasn't going to work because he wasn't getting paid. I pointed out to him that he had committed fraud and that the Marine Corps was housing and feeding him. I asked him to reconsider, but he was adamant. I called the brig warden and told him the story, and he told me to send the man over. When the man got there he repeated to the brig warden the same thing he had told me. The warden looked at him and said, "It's all right if you don't want to work. Just go get in that cell, but you won't get anything to eat until you change your mind." He missed one meal and then decided to go along with the program. We got lots of misfits. Recruiters had to make a quota, and they accepted people who were not qualified.

86

Lack of Housing and Interesting Events at Parris Island

The worst thing about Parris Island was the lack of housing for married personnel. There was supposed to be a one-year waiting list, and it was hard to find anyplace to live. Our first place was formerly a tenant house. The owner said she rented it out to help the men in service, but she had not done anything to fix the place up. There was no heat, and we had to cook on a kerosene stove. We had friends on the base, and we visited them to get warm and take a bath. It was an unusually cold winter. We finally found a room we could rent in Beaufort, a nearby town. It was in an old house in the historical district. It wasn't ideal, but it was better than being in the old tenant house on Ladys Island.

I had one sergeant who carried prisoners to Portsmouth, Virginia. I had known him previously in the Fourth Marines. *He had been a drill instructor, but one day he got angry with his men about something. He had them line up, and he hit each one on the head with his little swagger stick. He then asked the men if he had skipped anyone. One little recruit held up his hand and said, "Sir, you didn't hit me." The sergeant went over and rapped him on his head. The sergeant told me this story, and then he asked me, "Do you know what happened then? He was the only one who reported me, and I was taken off the job and reprimanded." It probably cost him a promotion.*

Before I came to Parris Island there had been a general's wife who had allergies. She blamed it on the ragweed. She decided to do something about it, so one day she ordered Operation Ragweed. She had everyone on the base out pulling up ragweed. There were no exceptions, from colonels down to privates.

87

Transporting Prisoners to Portsmouth, Virginia; To Marine Corps Headquarters to Ask for Transfer

I got myself put on the list to take two prisoners to Portsmouth Naval Prison. I did this because I wanted to go to Marine Corps headquarters and get a transfer to another base or overseas. I did not believe I was going to find a decent place to live anywhere close to the base. After a year on the base housing list I wasn't close to getting anything on the base. Another marine and I picked up the prisoners and boarded a train for Portsmouth, Virginia. I never knew the nature of their offenses. Every place we went, people were glaring at us. The prisoners were young and innocent-looking and we were wearing pistols and the two men were handcuffed. When we boarded the train the handcuffs had to be removed. This was because if there was a wreck they might be trapped. We had tickets for their meals, and we let them order from the menu. That night, we put them in the uppers in the Pullman. They had to take off all their clothing and pass it down to us. If they tried to escape they would be in the nude. We took turns staying awake, but they didn't try to make a break. We turned them over to the prison officials.

The next day we went to Marine Corps headquarters. I went in to talk to the enlisted detail officer. He was polite but he said that it was the policy to stay two to two and one-half years at a post. We hung around Washington for a couple of days and then took the train back to Parris Island.

88

We Buy a Home in Beaufort, near Parris Island

I decided that I would buy a house. My wife had not complained, but she deserved something better. We found a nice place in a good part of town. We bought it and moved in. My youngest sister was working for civil service on the base and living with us. I thought we would be there for a year or so, and I planted a garden and worked on improving the lawn. My mother came to visit, and when she saw me planting a garden she told me it wouldn't grow because I planted it on Sunday. My brother and his wife and my mother and father came to visit right after Elaine and I moved in. We had just moved and had not finished furnishing the place. We only had one bed, so my parents got the bed and the rest of us had to sleep on the floor. The next morning, my father said, "I couldn't sleep a wink," and my sister remarked, "Then you should have gotten up and let somebody else have the bed." I think he probably slept some, but he didn't like to be away from home. I don't think he ever got more than two hundred miles away from where he was born. He was anxious to leave, and he said, "Let's go home. I've seen the place." But the others wanted to stay another day. I went out to the base and got some cots so we all had something to sleep on that night.

After Elaine and I got some furniture and got settled, I cut some wood for the fireplace and thought we would be there for at least a year, but the first of November I got orders for Camp LeJeune, North Carolina. It was probably the largest post in the Marine Corps. We put our house up for sale. A man bought it, but I had problems getting paid. I finally went back to Beaufort and told the buyer I would get a lawyer and sue him if he did not finish paying for the place. He managed to get the balance. Elaine and I loaded the car and drove to Myrtle Beach the next day. At that time the place closed down in the winter, but there was one motel open. We got to Camp Lejeune the next day and reported in.

*   *   *

Part XI

89

Stationed at Camp Lejeune, North Carolina—1948

The housing situation was as bad here as at Parris Island. We stayed a few nights in an old trailer, but we didn't unload the car. We saw an ad in the paper about some rooms in town. We met the people who wanted to rent the rooms. They had some rules about the place. We would have to live with the old father and go to bed at ten o'clock at night, and no alcohol was allowed. We didn't like this arrangement. A couple we had known for years had a house near the base, and they took us in until we could get a place of our own. We had heard stories for years about Camp Lejeune. Most people did not like the place. It was far away from any city that had any night life for the young single men. For married personnel, though, it was good except for the weather in summer. There were good beaches. There was excellent hunting and fishing. The base had two golf courses, PXs and a commissary, restaurants, and bowling alleys. After we got government housing we seldom went off the base. When we could get a long weekend we would drive to South Carolina to visit our folks. This time I wasn't in the FMF. The FMF spent lots of time in the field or in Puerto Rico. It was part of what is now called the Rapid Deployment Force. You had to be ready to ship out in a matter of hours and might be out for several weeks. The base personnel didn't go anywhere. It was a lot like having a civilian job.

I ended up as first sergeant of a camp motor transport company. The men worked with civilian personnel, and some of the company got to looking like civilians. The company commander told me his main concern was motor transport and that I would be responsible for personnel. It took a while, but I got them back to looking like marines. I believe we were the first company to integrate with the black troops. It went over reasonably well, but if things didn't go to suit the blacks some of them claimed they were being discriminated against. One went to see the commanding general and said that he should have been promoted to corporal and that we were prejudiced. Naturally the company commander was concerned by this charge, and he asked me why the man had not been promoted. I got out the man's service record and showed the captain that he had failed to pass the examination. This relieved his mind, but he was really mad. He had me bring the man into the office and pointed out to him why he had not made corporal and then he laid the law down. He told him that if he went to see the general again he would have him locked up. He used very forcible language. The man was afraid to try anything like that again.

I traded rides with a master sergeant, and we got in the habit of stopping by the Staff NCO Club and would end up a couple of hours late getting home. This caused the wives to be upset, and each wife blamed the other's husband for the delay. I stopped one day to pick him up and he wasn't there, but one of the kids started hollering, "Mama, that damn old Wright is here!" I knew where he had heard that before.

I was in Camp Lejeune about a year, and it was good duty. We had lots of friends. I hunted and fished, and in the summer we spent lots of time at the beach. We had a house near the main gate and a short drive to my office.

90

To Dayton, Ohio, for I and I Duty

I went to work one morning and the post sergeant major called me and said I had orders to go to Dayton, Ohio, and form a reserve battalion. I had never had what was called I and I duty. The I and I was inspector and instructor. I expected to report to a unit that was already in operation, but we had to start from scratch—just another empty building. There was a major and three of us NCOs to start forming the unit.

Once again we started looking for a place to live. We found a room and my wife found a place in the wrong end of town. It was an upstairs apartment, and we settled in and got our furniture out of storage. We were out a distance from the center of town, but there was bus service. After a while I was in a car pool.

We had an outstanding officer, the CO of the reserve unit. He had led an infantry battalion in World War II but had left the service when the war ended. There was no problem in filling up the battalion with officers and senior NCOs. All of them had served in World War II. It took longer to enlist the lower ranks, and they had not had service before.

I disliked paperwork. All of my promotions had been in the line. I had never worked in an office, and I had always had competent personnel to do clerical work. We only had two hours a week to work with the reservists to complete records and reports. There was no way to keep up, and it was very frustrating. Also, I missed being away from the regular Marine Corps.

We kept recruiting members and in June we went to Quantico, Virginia, for reserve training. While we were there the reserves operated as a battalion and the I and I staff were observers. We were camped out near Manassas, a few miles from the base.

We had been in camp a week when the North Koreans invaded South Korea. We finished the two weeks' training and flew back to Dayton, Ohio. A few days later the battalion was ordered for active duty. We had to get them equipped for movement to the West Coast. The battalion was about half-strength, but they got ready to board a train. They marched from the reserve center to the railway station. The wives and kids were crying and trying to hold onto their men. The march finally broke up, but they all got aboard the train. They had not expected to leave home when they joined the reserves, and it caused real hardship when the breadwinners had to go away. I had never seen anything like this. In the regular Marine Corps we and our wives were accustomed to separations. We considered it a part of our jobs. (*I heard later that when they got to Camp Pendleton, California, the battalion was disbanded and the men were transferred to infantry units and shipped overseas. They should have had more training before they shipped out. Some of the men didn't know how to load a rifle.*) We stayed in Dayton until we could get rid of what was left behind.

91

To Camp Lejeune for a Month and Then to Camp Pendleton, Return to South Carolina for My Father's Funeral, December 1950

I requested duty overseas, but I got orders to Camp Lejeune. I was there about a month when they ordered me to Camp Pendleton to an amphibian tractor maintenance school. While I was at Camp Pendleton I got word that my father was dying. The family knew his condition was critical and had been expecting him to die before this. He was sixty-nine years old and had had cancer for several months. I took leave and traveled on space available, but I got stranded in Pensacola, Florida. I finished up the rest of the way by train. I met a cousin when I got to Anderson, South Carolina. He told me that my father had died and was being buried that same day. I got a ride out to the church and joined a group that was on the way to the graveside services. The funeral services had already been held inside the church and everyone had about given up on my arriving in time for the burial. I went home with my family but only stayed a few days. I got back to Camp Pendleton and finished up with the rest of the class. Since I was on temporary duty from Camp Lejeune I had to return there. This time we got housing in just a few days.

92

Maneuvers to Puerto Rico

I was back in the battalion about a month when we went on maneuvers to Puerto Rico. We traveled on an LSD (Landing Ship Dock). In the past I was usually making landings on LSDs. This was a landing ship for tanks or trucks. The LSD was a big improvement over the LST. The LST had to go all the way to shore and lower a ramp to unload. This meant they were exposed to enemy fire at close range. The LSD could unload the amphibian tractors away from the beach by flooding the deck and driving them off the ship. Troops could load in amphibian tractors while still on board. This meant no time was lost in transporting the men from the ships' boats, and when they got to the shore they could move directly inland and reduce the chances of getting knocked off when they got ashore. The LSD was roomy and when the water was pumped out the men could stay on their vehicles if they wanted to.

Staff NCOs had comfortable living quarters. It was almost like a cruise ship compared to what we had been accustomed in World War II. We had been at sea for about three days when we celebrated the Marine Corps birthday on the tenth of November. This is the biggest event of the year for all marines. The navy cooperated with a fine dinner and the birthday cake. Tradition calls for the oldest marine to cut the cake with a sword and give the first piece to the youngest marine. I found out at age thirty-six that I was the oldest marine aboard. The Marine Corps messages were read, and I cut the cake and handed the piece to the youngest private, who was probably about seventeen years old.

We arrived in Vieques, Puerto Rico, and made operations from the ship and did not set up camp ashore. *I had made two operations here in the 1930s, which was over twelve years before.* They were known as FLEX, or Fleet Landing Exercises. After we were there a few days I got a chance to visit the little town of Isabel Segunda. It looked about like it did years earlier. *When I was there before I had met a schoolteacher and her daughter. I remembered where she lived and stopped by to see them. The daughter was a beautiful girl of about eighteen years of age, and I believe she was an only child and her father was dead. She met and married a serviceman, and they moved to New York. She died the first winter she was there.* I felt really sad for the mother, but I think it had happened several years before.

93

Return to Camp Lejeune/Commissioned as Second Lieutenant

We completed the exercises and returned to Camp Lejeune and landed on the beach. It was after dark when we got ashore. We didn't try to get back to the barracks. It was late, and the temperature was below freezing. We spent a cold night on the beach in the vehicles and moved back to battalion headquarters the following day. The battalion commander recomended me for a commission. I didn't believe that at my age and without a college degree I would be considered, and I was satisfied to be an NCO. I finally got orders for Korea and reported in at Camp Pendleton. I was assigned to a draft that was supposed to leave in a few days. Two days before going to San Diego to go aboard ship I was notified that I had been commissioned as a second lieutenant. I was duly sworn in and then was told that I had been removed from the orders for overseas. I got assigned duty as an infantry instructor. We were training the men in the weapons they would use overseas. It was good duty and I was home most nights. My wife was still with me, but we had stored our furniture, expecting that I would go to Korea as soon as we arrived on the West Coast.

Commissioned as Second Lt. William J. Wright, 1952

94

Orders to Korea

After about a month I had not received orders and I went to see the colonel who was in charge of amphibian tractors. I had served in his battalion during World War II. I told him my story and asked if he could get me orders for Korea. This was on Tuesday and he said, "If you haven't heard anything by Friday, call me." My orders came on Thursday, and I reported to Department of Pacific, San Francisco. My orders called for air transportation. When we checked in I met the personnel officer. He told me I could stay a few days before going overseas. I asked him to give me three days. My wife was still with me, and she wanted to sell the car and fly back to her parents' home in Ohio. We went to a dealer and sold the car. She returned home and I went to Travis Air Force Base and boarded a plane for Hawaii.

95

To Hawaii, Kwajalein, Johnston, and Guam

The plane I was on was an earlier model, and it had to stop and refuel often. I was on the orders with a captain and a full colonel. A colonel is a VIP. Every time we stopped anywhere, a vehicle with a driver was waiting. We flew all night and arrived in the morning. I had seen Diamond Head before but had never flown over it. I thought it was a solid rock, but I could see the large hole where the volcano had been. I stayed in the officers' guest house. It was downtown and close to everything. That night we went to a Chinese restaurant. I don't know the correct spelling of the name, but it sounded like "Lousy Chow." It turned out to be good food and entertainment. The next night we went to Trader Vic's, a well-known place at that time. I felt out of place being out with a colonel, but he was a real gentleman and it didn't seem to bother him. Again I knew the personnel officer. He had been a sergeant major before he was commissioned. He asked me if I wanted to stay around for a few days. I declined and continued on with the colonel.

We flew to Kwajalein, Johnston, and Guam. We sat on canvas seats and had bologna sandwiches. On Kwajalein we ate at the mess hall. Everyone lined up and carried trays. The airstrip took up most of the island. It was a desolate place. I was glad I wasn't on a place like that; I would rather be in Korea. The next afternoon we landed on Guam. *I had been there with the Third Marine Division in World War II and had stopped there on the way to China and on the way back.* The commanding officer of the base met us and asked if anyone wanted to see the island, stating that if he did the CO would furnish a jeep and driver. It was hot and humid, and none of us chose to go. We could see the officers' club with air-conditioning and food and cold drinks. We thought we would be there only a few hours, but after we were in the air for an hour or so something went wrong with a generator and we returned to Guam and spent the night. If I had known we were going to be there, I would have opted for the tour. I would like to have seen some of the natives I had met when I was there before.

96

We Land in Japan

We got a good night's sleep and took off for Japan. We flew over Iwo Jima. It didn't look like much from the air, but the name was well known because of the picture of the flag-raising and as a place where six thousand marines and twenty thousand Japanese died. We landed in Japan before dark. We could see the famous Mt. Fuji. We had a three day-delay. The first night we went out to a Japanese restaurant. I had been to them in China, before the war, but this one was more elaborate. They knelt and removed our shoes and kept bowing until we got to the table. A couple of the waitresses were widows. Their husbands had been killed in the Solomon Islands. They wanted to know where we had served. They didn't seem to be angry with Americans. We could go anywhere at night and feel safe. The men didn't show any signs of resentment. *The people we talked to thought that the fire bombs had killed more people than the atomic bombs. We didn't see any damage caused by the war. This was seven years later, and everything seemed normal.* We stayed at the BOQ, and when we went to the shower we had to share it with the maids who were doing the ironing. Being in a room with naked men did not seem to bother them. They also took baths together. We spent a couple of days looking around, and then we boarded the plane for Korea.

97

In Korea

We landed at the airport in Korea and looked around. There were only a few buildings in Seoul that had not been flattened, and the ones still standing were in bad shape. We got in trucks and drove a few miles to a temporary station. As we drove through the countryside we could see women washing clothes in the streams. They were bare from the waist up and had a bunch of little children with them. The farmers were out in the fields working. They had used human waste on their crops and this could be detected a mile up in the air. Some of us who had been in China pretended we enjoyed the aroma. A young chaplain with us was dumbfounded. I don't know if he believed us or not. The next day we got to division headquarters and were assigned in the various units. The war ended up like World War I. The people on the front lines were dug in. They had trenches and fortifications with barbed wire and sandbags.

I was sent to amphibian tractors battalion headquarters. They assigned me to a company out on Kimpo Peninsula. It was over twenty miles from the other units and the only company still operating amtracs. The other companies had turned their vehicles over to battalion headquarters and had taken up positions along the Imjan River. We operated in the river, and sometimes we would go all the way to Inchou. It was an old town and had not been damaged as much as Seoul. The hospital ship was tied up there, and people who were wounded could be aboard ship in a very short time. I went to the ship to pay one of our men. I talked to a nurse, and she said her job was to clean up the patients for an operation. Some of them were in really bad shape. Helicopters would fly the patients in on stretchers tied onto the helicopters. The army had what they called a MASH. The television series by that name played for a long time.

One day I was walking along the road near our camp and met an old Korean man who was smoking a long-stemmed pipe. I asked him to let me look at it, and he did. After looking it over, I gave it back to him. Then he asked me if he could look at my pipe, a Kaywoodie that was well broken in and one of my favorites. I handed it to him, and he stuck it in his toothless mouth. I took it away from him but then decided I couldn't smoke it again, and I gave it back to him. As he grinned, I knew he had just pulled a fast one on me.

There was a small village near camp, and they would scrounge anything we threw away. They would take beer cans and make cups, or they would straighten out the cans and use them for shingles. We had a dump where we buried garbage. They would dig it up. This upset the commander, and he had the head man brought into company headquarters. The commander told him that if they didn't stop it he would take a bulldozer and push the village off the cliff. This worked for a few days, and then they were back doing the same thing again.

The children were bright and the little girls were pretty. They had almost nothing to play with, but I believe they were happier than American children. They would skip rope and sing. The little girls were baby-sitters. Most of them had a baby strapped onto her back. I had always heard that you had to be careful in handling babies, but these little girls apparently had not been told about this. They skipped rope with the babies on their backs, and the little heads flopped every which way. In the winter they played outdoors and didn't seem to mind the cold. They wore rubber shoes without socks, just some grass stuffed around their feet. The farmers had to do everything the hard way. I saw a couple of men shoveling water uphill. They had something like a trough. It was mounted on a tripod. They would move the water up to the next terrace. They kept the fields flooded during the growing season. They had oxen to plow up the fields before planting, but other than that everything was done by hand. They planted each stalk of rice by hand and harvested it with a scythe. They stacked the rice in bundles and used oxen to thrash the grain.

One day a Korean officer stopped by the company. The captain invited him to have lunch with us. A chaplain was there and someone asked the Korean officer what he was going to do with the North Korean spy he had caught the night before. He said, "We will interrogate him and execute him." The chaplain thought the North Korean should have a trial. The Orientals have a different way of doing things. The prisoner had North Korean money in his pocket, and I'm not sure what other proof they had. I imagine he told them all he knew during the interrogation.

I thought I was settled for the rest of my tour, which was about a year, but in October I was transferred to battalion headquarters. I preferred being in a company, but the battalion was back from the front quite a ways and there was more going on than in the company. My job was to maintain the amtracs and have them ready to move if necessary. I had over a hundred vehicles and about a hundred men. The senior NCOs were all career men who had served in World War II. When I took over I found out that the captain I relieved had put staff NCOs in the tents with the lower ranks. I allowed the senior men to have tents apart from the lower enlisted grades. I think this one particular move got me off on the right foot with the men, and we had a good winter. We were seldom bothered by anyone from the battalion.

98

We go to Japan for R and R

In December I went to Japan with a group for R and R (Rest and Relaxation). We went to Kyoto. It was a historical city and had been the capital in the early days. I told the men when to be back and let them go. I checked into a good hotel. I had a good meal and decided to go to a bathhouse. The water was hot, but it didn't seem to bother the local people. Some were there with their families. I had planned to go out and look around, but after the bath I just wanted to go to sleep. The next day I went to a Japanese opera. The girls had elaborate costumes and might have been pretty, but their faces were covered with some kind of white paint. I didn't think much of the music, and I dozed off. A woman seated nearby woke me and said in English, "How can you spend so much money to see the show and then sleep?" I told her it was because I had been in Korea and had not been warm.

I decided I wanted to see Tokyo and bought a train ticket in the lobby of the hotel. It was going to be an overnight trip and I wanted a sleeper, but something was going on in the capital and no sleepers were available. I got on the train and spoke to the conductor about a place to sleep, and he said there wasn't any. I offered him fifty yen and he must have chased somebody out, because in a little while he found a place for me. I arrived in Tokyo, got a hotel, and then went sightseeing. The main thoroughfare was crowded with people, and there were cafés filled up with women. Some of them had had an operation on their eyes to make them less slanted. They had a game called Pachinko that they liked to play. Some of the performers were dressed like American cowboys and were trying to sing in English, but they couldn't pronounce the words properly.

The next day I got a cab to take me to the Emperor's Palace. We drove around the grounds, but we didn't see any of the royal family or the emperor's white horse. Admiral Halsey had said that he was going to ride the horse when we got to Japan, but he didn't. When I returned to the hotel I placed a telephone call to my wife. We could not understand each other very well, and it made me miss her more. I didn't make any more calls.

I rode the train back to Kyoto and did some shopping. They would mail the goods back for us. Prices were reasonable and I should have bought more. When we got ready to return to Korea everyone was present. They had enjoyed the time spent in Japan, but they were ready to go back to Korea.

In May we got orders to move to a place called Ascom City. It was a rear base and was near Inchow. They were meeting with North Koreans and trying to get something worked out. A small North Korean plane would fly over at night, but I don't think he did much damage.

99

Rotated Back to the United States

People who had been in Korea about a year were being rotated back to the USA. I got orders along with a group of people from division headquarters. We rode an LST out to the ship and went aboard. The ship had been a passenger ship before the war, and the accommodations were very good. We made it back in seventeen days. We made the northern circle route and got up near the Aleutians before turning south. It was foggy most of the time. We landed in San Francisco, and when we passed under the Golden Gate Bridge the sun was shining.

We pulled up to the dock, and my wife was waiting with a new car. I had a chance to greet her and tell her I would see her that night. We had to go to Treasure Island to get processed and pick up orders. I knew the sergeant major at Treasure Island. He got me through in a hurry, but I had to go back the next day.

My wife and I stayed in San Francisco three days. I had thirty days' leave, so we didn't need to rush. My nephew was a sailor, and he was aboard ship at Oakland. I called him, and he came over for a visit. We saw a play, *Guys and Dolls*, and visited a couple of night spots. I had a brother in Whittier, California, and we drove down the coastal highway. We took our time and stopped one night on the way. We visited my brother and his family and toured around the area. We saw Disney Land and the Farmers Market and the Old Mission at San Juan Capistrano.

After a few days, we headed east. We got to Las Vegas about the middle of the day, and it was so hot that we started looking for a motel that had air-conditioning and a swimming pool. It was a little cooler that night, and we went out to eat and to a casino. My wife had never played craps, and she had beginner's luck. She won enough to pay for the meal and the motel room. We followed Route 66 all the way to Oklahoma and then headed east to South Carolina. My father had died before I went to Korea, but my mother and some of my family still lived near the home place.

*   *   *

Part XII

100

Back at Camp Lejeune, North Carolina

When my leave was up we reported to Camp Lejeune. It was almost like coming home. I knew most of the officers. Two of them had been in the company with me in Korea. Everything was better this time. I got housing near the base and got on the list for government quarters. I was promoted to first lieutenant and was a company executive officer. I was number two in the company. A year later I was promoted to captain and was given command of a company. I liked being company commander, and I believe I was good at the job. I liked saying, "First Sergeant, take a note," and saying, "Order my jeep." I had been enlisted for most of my career, and I knew all the excuses and alibis. I also knew that the men should get credit when they did a good job. Also, a good NCO doesn't have to be told how to do his job.

When I took over the company they needed a little more discipline. We went to a battalion parade and on the way back they talked in ranks and straggled. When we got back to the barracks they expected to halt and fall out, but we didn't stop. I ordered them to continue to march and took them back to the parade ground. I halted them and told them that if they didn't square away I would have close order drill every day. I also told the senior NCOs that I expected more out of them. I didn't criticize the NCOs in front of the troops. When we had inspections the company would fall out an hour or more before the inspection party arrived.

I told them I wouldn't have them standing and waiting if they would get ready while they were inside. Also, NCOs would check them before they fell out. This worked fine and I think the troops appreciated it.

I always felt bad when I had to take a man to the colonel for office hours. I would think that I should have tried harder to straighten them out, but I had one man who didn't try to get along. He was AWOL several times. I had tried to talk to him and had given him company punishment, but nothing worked. Finally he got sent to the brig for thirty days. I didn't expect to see him for a while, but they had a policy that a prisoner could request to see his company commander while serving sentence. I drove across camp to see him, and I asked him about his problem. He said that he didn't like being locked up and he didn't like the other prisoners. Then he said his girlfriend was supposed to visit him and now that it was summer he would like to spend some time at the beach. I reminded him that he had brought it all on himself and that he didn't deserve any favors. I told him I didn't want to see him again while he was locked up.

A few of the married men had been getting a half-day off during the week to do something with their wives. They would claim they had to drive their wives to the commissary or hospital. It seemed that none of the wives could drive. I questioned the men and listened to their stories, and then I told them they could have the time off, but they would have to come in on Saturday and report to the police sergeant for a working party. Almost all of them decided they didn't have to have time off during the week. A couple of them really did have problems, and I let them go as usual.

101

Good Housing, Comfortable Life, and Getting Ready to Retire—1956

This was the first time my wife and I had quarters on base, and we had a large comfortable house. We knew lots of people. My wife played golf and joined a bridge club. This would be the longest time we had spent at any station. We had moved fifteen times since we were married.

Our operations were mainly on the base. There was plenty of room for training the men. We practiced landings on the beach, and two or three times a year we went aboard ship. We went back to Puerto Rico, and in the summer we operated around Norfolk, Virginia. We carried out operations with the naval cadets from the academy. I had in almost twenty years in 1956.

I planned to retire, and I had bought a rundown farm near my family in South Carolina. It had been farmed by tenants, and they had not been interested in making improvements. Another reason for retiring was that I was old for my rank and I had not been to college. A group came to Camp Lejeune from Marine Corps headquarters and had all officers assemble in the camp theater. They told us there would be 50 percent attrition for promotion to major from captain. I figured this would eliminate me. I felt very fortunate to have held a commission. I had not finished high school, although I had passed the high school equivalency test. Also, I had talked to some of the officers who had stayed in for thirty years and they said it was better to go out while you were still young and could get a job or start a business. I knew that I wanted to go back to the farm. When I left the farm at age seventeen I had no intention of ever farming again. I had seen how bad hard times could be. At this time, though, I would have retirement pay and I wouldn't grow cotton.

Commissioned Capt. William J. Wright, 1956.

102

I Am Requested to Take a Company to the Suez Canal, but All We Did Was Sail up and down the Virginia Coast

You could put in your letter for retirement three months in advance. I requested to be separated in January 1957. A few days later the battalion commander called for me to come to his office. He wanted to know if I would delay my retirement and take a company to the Suez Canal. There was fighting going on, and we would help evacuate Americans if it became necessary. I don't know why he wanted me to go, because most of the officers wanted to take part, especially the ones who had not been in World War II. I could have refused, but I had always gone whenever I was requested. We assembled at the beach and waited for the LST to pick us up. I don't know what was wrong with the captain of the ship, but he wouldn't come near the beach and we had to go out about a mile to get aboard. He was a young officer, and maybe he was afraid of getting his ship stuck on the way in. The commanding general, by the nickname of Loopy, had put out an order that the next officer who lost an amphibian tractor would be court-martialed. The water was rough, but we all got aboard and sailed for Norfolk, Virginia. We expected to join a convoy and go overseas. We waited for days, always expecting to get orders, and after a while we left port, but all we did was sail up and down the coast. I had the troop commander's quarters. They were as good as the ones occupied by the ship's captain. For meals I was seated on the captain's right side and could sit on the ship's bridge after years of being down in the ship's hold. It was nice to travel like this. We kept sailing up and down the coast and would put in at Norfolk occasionally.

103

Retirement from USMC–1957

One day I got word unofficially that we were not going anywhere. I went to Headquarters FMF Atlantic and asked for
a ride on a plane to Marine Corps headquarters. I got a ride
the next day to Washington. The plane had only four seats.
We flew through snow all the way, and when I arrived I went
to Marine Corps headquarters and asked to be put back on
the retirement list. A woman who worked in the department
told me she could get me back on the list to retire in January
1957. If I had waited one more day, I would not have been
able to make it and would have had to start over. I returned
to the ship and found that the rumor was correct. We got
orders to return to Camp Lejeune. We landed on the beach
and then proceeded back to the barracks. It was about the
middle of December, and I was relieved and did not have
any further duties. Our furniture had to be shipped, but it
wasn't difficult because the Marine Corps does the packing
and shipping.

I had to have a physical examination. A young navy
doctor examined me, and he seemed frustrated when he
could not find any problems. I was forty-one years old, and
that is old for a junior officer in the Marine Corps. He said,
"Captain, one of these days you are going to fall apart like
the one-horse-shay." I would go out to the battalion each
morning, so they would know I was still around.

Now that I was leaving, I became more popular. The
men threw a party for me and presented me with fishing

gear. The officers had one and put on a dinner and dance at the main club. It was a nice party, and when the band played "Auld Lang Syne" everyone left the floor except my wife and me. It was the end of twenty years' service, some good and some bad. I had enlisted as a private and was retiring as a captain.

Enlisting in the Marine Corps was one of the best things that ever happened to me. I had not finished high school and had been drifting around the country for four years before entering the service. I had crossed the country several times. I had worked in the fields out west and sold magazine subscriptions door to door. I had ridden freight trains across the country. I had been put in jail a few times for trespassing on railroad property or just being rounded up by police to see if they could catch a criminal. In the Marine Corps I had scubbed floors, but I also had the honor to become an officer.

After the parties they asked me if I wanted a parade held for me. Some people refused to have a ceremony, but I decided to go all the way. My wife was dressed in her best outfit, wearing an orchid, and looking beautiful. I wasn't expecting anyone except our people, but Gen. Jack Juhan came down from force troops. He was called Smiling Jack, a real officer and gentleman. We had our pictures taken with him. Many years later I sent him one of the pictures, and although he was about ninety years old by that time, he wrote and thanked me.

On the day of the parade it had rained and the ground was wet. The ceremony was held in the battalion area. The general and I trooped the line and inspected the troops. After that I spoke to a few people and then my wife and I got in the car and started out for the farm. I had a sister in Georgetown, South Carolina, and we stopped to visit them on the way home. We stayed another day with them and went to a dance the next night. It was the last time I would wear the uniform of the United States Marines.

*   *   *

Honorable William J. Wright, South Carolina House of Representatives, 1962

Epilogue

I want to borrow a phrase from a marine comrade who was nicknamed Azee. His real name started with an *A* and ended with a Z, with many letters in between, hence the nickname. When everybody else was griping about something, Azee would come up with his favorite expression, *It coulda been a tousand times vorser.*" Yes, indeed, in looking back over my life I must say, "It could have been a thousand times worse."

My parents raised nine children without the help of Dr. Spock. I don't think they wasted any time analyzing whether they were doing the right thing or not, and we kids didn't have time to sit around wondering if we were being treated fairly. We didn't recognize that we were poor because our relatives and neighbors were in the same boat.

I loved reading and although books were scarce in our home and school, I managed to find papers, magazines, comic books, and wild western books. I began to dream about traveling. Working in the cotton fields with the sun beating down I had plenty of time to dream and fantasize about traveling. Before I was twenty-one my wish had come true and my travels had taken me all across the United States and part of Canada.

I had a good career and took pride in coming up through the ranks of the enlisted to become a captain in the U.S. Marines. After retirement I served two terms in the House of Representatives. I had the freedom to farm and dabble in real estate and still have time for fishing and golf and friends.

The best thing that happened was meeting a beautiful young lady named Elaine Hyde. She was from Ohio and I from South Carolina, and we met in Florida. We have celebrated fifty-nine years of marriage. She has been a partner every step of the way. She was the perfect military wife, accepting each tour of duty as it came and always taking care of the home front while I was away. She was a city girl, but after retirement she became a terrific farmer's wife. She has been my bridge partner, golf partner, and traveling companion. How glad I am that we just happened to be in the same place at the same time in 1941.

338 - 0600